About the

Amory Sta...
documenta...
Naming the
Movements
Books, 200

AMORY STARR

Global revolt

A guide to the movements against
globalization

Photos by Tim Russo, independent
media activist

Zed Books
LONDON | NEW YORK

Global revolt: A guide to the movements against globalization was first published in 2005, by Zed Books Ltd, 7 Cynthia Street, London N1 9JF, UK and Room 400, 175 Fifth Avenue, New York, NY 10010, USA

www.zedbooks.co.uk

Cover designed by Andrew Corbett
Cover images, top: www.undercurrents.org.; bottom: Zula Lucerno
Set in Arnhem and Futura Bold by Ewan Smith, London
Printed and bound in Malta by Gutenberg Press Ltd

Distributed in the USA exclusively by Palgrave Macmillan, a division of St Martin's Press, LLC, 175 Fifth Avenue, New York, NY 10010.

A catalogue record for this book is available from the British Library.
US CIP data are available from the Library of Congress.

ISBN 1 84277 482 4 hb
ISBN 1 84277 483 2 pb

Contents

For I-ya and all the grandmothers,
with intransigence

1 | Introduction: another world *is* possible – how do we know?

Global elites, their political henchmen and media sycophants insist that economic growth, international trade, the elimination of subsidies and privatization will alleviate poverty. Activists' blossoming confidence that another world is possible is well-rooted. Analysis of the effects of structural adjustment and free trade policies reveal that their promises are unfulfilled. Indeed, their impact has been perverse. Apparently, globalization works only for the rich. Even high-profile administrators of neoliberalism have deserted. Their insider revelations[1] are hardly news to the non-governmental organizations which had been carefully collecting data for decades.[2] Inequality has increased in nearly every country; internationally,[3] the conditions of life for the poor and indigenous peoples have steadily deteriorated; and the environment on which we all depend has been irrevocably damaged.

In what ought to be the invitation to its formal suicide, the World Bank admits that its structural adjustment programmes undermine its core economic shibboleth: economic growth. Damning also is the collapse of the obedient 'developing nations' of South-East Asia and Latin America, as well as the failure of the command-capitalist South Korean regime (the only country *ever* to graduate from 'Third' to 'First World' status). The evidence has accumulated to the point that, for those familiar with it, there is little further to be discussed. The holy trinity of export/trade/growth is exposed as a manipulative fraud and each new invocation of the dead and absurd promises of development – that it will bring peace, heal the environment or end poverty – is more transparent than the previous.[4] The economic and political system promoted by globalization is not only morally bankrupt, it is no longer credible as economics.

1 Zapatista members celebrate the first anniversary of the founding of their Caracoles, cultural centres of resistance, and the formation of the Councils of Good Governments in the rebel highlands village Oventic in Chiapas, Mexico, 8 August 2004 (photo by Tim Russo).

This book is intended to familiarize interested parties with the anti-globalization movement and to provide direction for further research and exploration of the 'movement of movements'. Because many exhaustive analyses of the machinations of globalization have already been written (you have probably read several of them) and because this book focuses on the resistance to globalization, this introduction will provide only a rudimentary review of the basis for opposition. Herewith, globalization's most egregious deceptions.

Globalization's thirteen biggest lies

1 *Globalization is old*   Globalization's marketing strategy steals the images of family, multiculturalism, communication, women's liberation, travel and trade and offers them back to us, glamorized and at a price. All of these things existed before colonialism and contested it at every stage of its development. These images obscure the structure of globalization, its macro-economic policies, and the corporate projects it promotes – all of which *damage* families, communication and culture. Describing itself as a 'constitution for a new global economy', the World Trade Organization (WTO) is designed to subvert existing international human rights and labour law, national sovereignty and parliamentary regulation. The highest international law (and the only enforceable one) is now 'free trade', a highly specified set of principles sometimes described as a 'bill of rights' for multinational corporations, multinational corporations, to which the laws of signatory countries are now secondary.

2 *Globalization is new* Globalization pretends to bring a new, 'rules-based', fairness and structure to the global trading system, but activists in the Global South call it 'recolonization'.[5] Not only does it force Third World nations to implement policies remarkably similar to those imposed by colonial administrations, it also reverses the gains of postcolonial governance in areas such as land reform, the nationalization of industries and cultural protections. Moreover, the 'free trade agreements', so

3

'new' that they have not yet been fully implemented, can already be evaluated by their predecessors of nearly two decades, the Structural Adjustment Programmes (SAPs) of the World Bank and the International Monetary Fund (IMF). The results of SAPs have been a steady increase in inequality[6] and the ruthless liquidation of economies to service the debt.

3 *Globalization may be exploitative or dislocating at the margins, but it's 'better than nothing' for the majority of the poor* Today's poor, and their regions, were self-sufficient for millennia. They were colonized for their mineral, timber, soil, human, animal and climatic wealth. The idea of a poor or hungry Africa or Asia or Latin America is absurd. Northerners who point to a line of people hoping for a job in a sweatshop and praise the Global North for generously providing jobs are peddling ahistoricism and paternalism.

Twenty years ago the people now queueing were independent small-scale producers, farmers, processors, craftspeople or artisans producing for local markets. Visitors depicted these sustainable livelihoods as backward and dirty, and leaders of Global South countries (already pummelled by centuries of their colonists' ethnocentric definitions of civilization) were seduced by visions of modernity.

Those appalled by pious arguments that slavery, despite its brutality, did a big favour to Africans (who at least were given the chance to become Christians and learn discipline) may soon find ourselves ashamed to have countenanced sweatshops, let alone congratulated the sweat-traders for 'providing jobs'. Neoliberal forms of development are never going to solve poverty, protect the environment or bring peace – these are dead promises. Instead, so-called 'development policies' primarily *benefit* global elites, at the cost of traditional, sustainable livelihoods, the local economies they support and the resources on which they depend.

4 *Globalization frees the market to satisfy important human needs* Human needs such as hunger are not a 'market demand'

4

– that is a privilege reserved for those whose needs and desires are backed by buying power. Since hungry people lack exactly that, a market-based food system will easily pass them by.[7] Instead of meeting human needs, neoliberalism invokes them as a façade while steadily undermining local provisioning.

Multinational corporations are able to profit from and intervene in local production through agricultural technology schemes which create dependency on expensive inputs. As postcolonial countries are pressured to export more to earn foreign exchange to pay their debts and to open their markets to imports, farmers simultaneously become dependent on volatile world prices while losing access to formerly protected, stable national markets. The same international trade system that promises 'cheap food' for the hungry and whose major players advertise their technologies and practices as absolutely essential to the task of 'feeding the world', in fact undermines national food production. The companies who make those promises undercut local producers with subsidized imports. As a result, nations lose food security and control over domestic food policy. Simultaneously, the WTO's SPS (Sanitary and Phyto-Sanitary) agreements undermine local value-added production by imposing sterilization and packaging standards which only multinational food corporations can afford. Meanwhile, artisans and craftspeople are undercut by low-quality mass-produced baubles whose only cultural value is a desperate scrap of Western style.

Aggressive marketing campaigns mobilize colonial ideology to manipulate food preferences and endanger local food cultures. Images of the Global South (particularly Africa) as 'hungry' are used to force biotechnology (a technology which has been rejected by farmers and consumers in the North) on Global South countries where farmers and consumers have made it clear they also do not want it.

5 *Globalization is about deregulation to 'free' the market from burdensome government regulations* Interestingly, globalization policies do not follow any classic economic orthodoxy.

They force *deregulation* when environmental protections, labour law or land reform are in the way of business operations. They force *regulation* to ensure patent payments or to create requirements that are cost-effective only for large-scale producers (handily disposing of competition from small, local competitors). These convoluted rules are designed to commodify life and then enable corporations to control and profit from trading the commodity.

6 *Globalization increases consumer choice* Citizens of most countries are demanding the right to choose whether or not they will eat biotech foods (genetically modified organisms, GMOs, or living modified organisms, LMOs). Most countries have some kind of label or restrictive scheme and the Biosafety Protocol recognizes countries' right to regulate their imports. But 'free trade' rules are rapidly overriding any legal invocation of the 'precautionary principle' which was, until recently, the basis of most law governing the marketing of new technologies.[8] Consumers receive the illusion of choice between brands and artificial flavours while choice over the more serious fundamentals, such as conditions of production, health risks and environmental impacts of products, are eliminated. In the end, the global market offers force not choice.

Even the most superficial consumer choices do not make it to the majority of the world, 2.8 billion of whom live on less than two dollars a day, which is the United Nations Development Programme's definition of absolute poverty and are losing control over the most basic choices as they are forced to migrate far from home and family to sell their love in the nanny market and their bodies in the sex trade.[9] Multinational corporations are exercising power not only to shape global, national and local economies, the concentration of wealth, the treatment of labour and political sovereignty, but also more *qualitative* aspects of life – defining science, shaping culture, standardizing and controlling our desires and definitions of dignity, delimiting public space and having no respect for the sacred.[10]

7 *Globalization is democratic* The World Bank and IMF evade mechanisms of international democracy by operating as 'proxy governments' of the USA, which controls the crucial proportion of votes.[11] WTO ministerials are collapsing not because elites of the Global South are unwilling to exploit their own people, but because these meetings are so undemocratic that they insult these elites and are politically untenable in sovereign postcolonial nations.[12] The WTO claims to work by consensus, but what that really means is simply that it will never allow voting, as the G8 (Group of Eight: the most powerful industrialized nations: France, Germany, Italy, Japan, the UK, the USA, Canada and Russia) would be outnumbered. The 'consensus process' – described as 'bullying' by Global South participants – is one in which documents are written by a small group dominated by G8 interests and then presented to the membership in a 'take it or leave it' manner.

'Free trade' policies violate (while trumping) a raft of putatively more democratic pieces of international law such as the UN Declaration of Human Rights, various conventions of the International Labor Organization, World Health Organization codes, and assorted environmental treaties.

Further undermining the very concept of democratic process, globalization labels as terrorism any refusal of its advances while subtly working to replace the values of citizenship with the values and 'rights' of consumerism.[13]

8 *Farmers and other small producers need access to global markets so they can 'compete'* Structural Adjustment Programmes and Free Trade Agreements (FTAs) mandate the elimination of tariffs on imports and any other supports to domestic producers in the Global South. Combined with the dumping of mass-produced and surreptitiously subsidized Global North exports, this results in the flooding of local markets with underpriced goods with which no small producer, however efficient and sustainable her operation, can compete (see point 4, above). Northern development experts patiently explain that this dumping will actually *stimulate* local producers

to awake from their stupor of backwardness and to become 'more competitive'. (In reality it wipes them out.)

9 *G8 countries and their institutions are trying to 'help' the poor nations and their peoples* International financial institutions (IFIs), such as the World Bank and the IMF, do not exist to make a monetary profit, but a profit of *control* over the economies of the Global South, facilitating G8 access to natural resources, land, labour and markets, just as in the colonial era. Meanwhile, foreign aid actually flows in reverse; there is a net outflow from South to North due to debt-servicing.[14]

Uprisings in the Global South have constantly been suppressed by regimes given extensive military backing by their former colonizers, and by newer imperial powers that feel entitled to sabotage sovereign democratic processes. Meanwhile, authentic grassroots development efforts are purposely derailed by incessant cooptation (even the World Bank now uses the language of 'participation').[15]

10 *Privatization is more efficient* Decades of ostensibly neutral policy analysts have relentlessly berated public ownership and administration for 'corruption' and 'inefficiency'. Maligning government as hopeless, this assault pre-empted opposition to the lucrative privatization of public resources and services. Privatization conveniently terminates civic scrutiny and accountability. From the perspective of Bolivians, South Africans and others on whom the deadly experiment of privatization of energy and water is being enacted, it is outright theft of their water, energy, national wealth and unionized industries.

11 *Global culture brings us all closer* 'Ancient blood feuds', 'tribal strife' and 'ethnic warfare', purportedly the inevitable result of an excess of heterogeneity, often turn out to be caused instead by the distortions of colonial land grabs, postcolonial borders and 'economic restructuring'.[16] The solutions offered by neoliberalism – homogenized corporate culture and expensive technology – benefit only their salesmen.

Corporate globalization tries to impose a standardized monoculture,[17] a brittle system. In contrast, the anti-globalization movement understands diversity to be the basis of security. In discovering and defending one another, the 'movement of movements' asserts Zapatista principles of '*un mundo donde quepan muchos mundos*' (a world where many worlds fit) and 'one no, many yeses'.

12 *There is no alternative (TINA)* This is the trump card of corporate power. Globalization is portrayed as natural, inevitable and the only form of progress. In fact, there are thousands of alternatives (TATA); and there must be an alternative (THEMBA).[18] The World Social Forum is one of many events at which people's movements confirm their collective wisdom, technology, skills, courage and ability to run things much better.

13 *Opponents of globalization are romantic Luddites,*[19] *alienated punk rock kids 'hopping' from summit to summit on 'protest tours'* These distorted images trivialize the suffering and rage of the working classes and youth of the North, where resistance movements are still marginal, but growing. The Global South is the real point of impact.

For decades, Global South farmers, small producers, students, consumers, workers, fisherfolk, urban dwellers, indigenous peoples, and the unemployed have been fighting back against neoliberal economic policies and generating alternatives. Since movements have discovered that formal political systems are collaborating with or being used by elites, new forms of power and spaces of democracy are being developed as bases for confrontation and to build 'another world'.

If any of these points were new to you, please see the Resources list and Notes at the end of this and every chapter.

Welcome to the revolt against globalization

What follows is a guidebook intended as an accessible introduction to the movement, not an evaluation or quantification of it. The book is organized in four sections. You should first read the bits that look helpful, and in any order you please.

Part One is a history of the formative threads of the revolt. This history deflates the myth that the movement began in the Global North (the First World) in 1999 at a protest in Seattle, and shows that the current movement emerged from the Global South (the Third World, postcolonial nations, or majority world) in a struggle that had been underway for nearly two decades prior to Seattle.

Part Two summarizes movement manifestos. While not exactly points of consensus, these are widely shared. Again, you will notice that most of the important manifestos were forged in the Global South. And you will notice that they take for granted neither the inevitability of globalization, nor the desirability of modernization, nor the forms of freedom pursued by postmodernists. This section presents these manifestos with respect and without external ideological litmus tests.

Part Three examines the major controversies, both ideological and strategic. Some of these are well known outside the movement, others are not. Some are high-profile debates, others are subterranean conflicts yet to be actively addressed.

Part Four introduces some of the most popular tactics of collaboration. The movements are diverse, dispersed and incredibly creative, so this is only a small sample of some of the more visible tactics. Please be aware that this tactical discussion is very basic and should not be used as a training manual, campaign blueprint or activist handbook. (Please do seek out some training.)

Another thing this book is not is a text of theory, fantasy or suggestion. Although it is written with exuberance intended to evoke the brightest moments of struggle, it is a distillation of the perspectives and positions of actual and active social movements. Commentary by non-activists has been assiduously disregarded. And the author, although industrious, lacks the imagination to have come up with any of this.

Resources

Colonialism Mark Cocker, *Rivers of Blood, Rivers of Gold: Europe's Conquest of Indigenous Peoples* (New York: Grove Press, 1998).

Growth Richard Douthwaite et al., *The Growth Illusion* (Gatariola Island, BC, Canada: New Society, 1992, 1999).

World Bank/structural adjustment Catherine Caufield, *Masters of Illusion: The World Bank and the Poverty of Nations* (New York: Henry Holt, 1997).

Jubilee Research: <www.jubilee2000uk.org>

Stephanie Black, *Life & Debt* (documentary film), 2001: <www.lifeanddebt.org>

Foreign aid David Sogge, *Give and Take: What's the Matter with Foreign Aid?* (London: Zed Books, 2002).

Free trade Lori Wallach and Patrick Woodall, *Whose Trade Organization? A Comprehensive Guide to the World Trade Organization,* 2nd edn (New York: New Press, 2004).

Global Trade Watch: <www.citizen.org/trade>

Sweatshops Ellen Israel Rosen, *Making Sweatshops: The Globalization of the US Apparel Industry* (Berkeley: University of California Press, 2002).

Kevin Bales, *Disposable People: New Slavery in the Global Economy* (Berkeley: University of California Press, 2000).

Sweatshop Watch with international links: <www.sweatshopwatch.org>

Privatization Vandana Shiva, *Water Wars* (Boston, MA: South End Press, 2002).

Maude Barlow and Tony Clarke, *Blue Gold: The Fight to Stop the Corporate Theft of the World's Water* (New York: New Press, 2002).

Saron Beder, *Power Play: The Fight to Control the World's Electricity* (New York: New Press, 2003).

Center for Public Integrity Water Barons page: <www.icij.org/water>

Biotech Mae-Wan Ho, *Genetic Engineering Dream or Nightmare?: The Brave New World of Bad Science and Big Business* (Bath: Gateway Books, 1998).

Bill Lambrecht, *Dinner at the New Gene Café* (New York: St Martin's Press, 2002).

Cultural imperialism John Tomlinson, *Cultural Imperialism: A Critical Introduction* (Baltimore, MD: Johns Hopkins University Press, 1991).

George Yúdice, *The Expediency of Culture* (Durham, NC: Duke University Press, 2003).

Globalization Robert Biel, *The New Imperialism: Crisis and Contradictions in North/South Relations* (London: Zed Books, 2000).

Edward Goldsmith and Jerry Mander (eds), *The Case Against the Global Economy and for a Turn Toward the Local* (London: Kogan Page, 2001).

Jim Yong Kim (ed.), *Dying for Growth: Global Inequality and the Health of the Poor* (Monroe, ME: Common Courage Press, 2000).

Patrick McCully, *Silenced Rivers: The Ecology and Politics of Large Dams* (London: Zed Books, 2001).

William J. Weinberg, *War on the Land: Ecology and Politics in Central America* (London: Zed Books, 1992).

Arundhati Roy, *The Cost of Living* (New York: Modern Library, 1999).

Joel Bakan, *The Corporation: The Pathological Pursuit of Profit and Power* (New York: Free Press, 2004).

Eduardo Galeano, *Upside Down: A Primer for the Looking Glass World* (New York: Henry Holt, 2000).

Walden F. Bello and Stephanie Rosenfeld, *Dragons in Distress: Asia's Miracle Economies in Crisis* (Oakland, CA: Food First Books, 1993).

Walden Bello (ed.), *Global Finance* (London: Zed Books, 2000).

Corporate Europe Observatory: <www.corporateeurope.org>

Third World Network: <www.twnside.org.sg>

WorldWatch Institute: <www.worldwatch.org>

Notes

1 Davison Budhoo, a senior economist with the IMF, resigned in May 1988; Joseph Stiglitz, senior vice president and chief economist at the World Bank, was forced to resign in 2000 for criticizing the IMF and World Bank; Clare Short, UK International Development Secretary, resigned on 5 December 2003; George Soros, billionaire philosopher, regularly publishes confirmation of the critiques of globalization made by activist critics.

2 Transnational Institute (founded 1974 <www.tni.org>); Institute for Food and Development Policy (founded 1975 <www.foodfirst.org>); World Development Movement (founded 1970 <www.wdm.org.uk>); International Rivers Network (founded 1985 <www.irn.org>).

3 UNDP 1999 *Human Development Report*. The income gap between the fifth of the world's people living in the richest coun-

tries and the fifth in the poorest grew to 74 to 1 in 1997, up from 60 to 1 in 1990 and 30 to 1 in 1960. Inequalities within countries have been rising too, even in Eastern Europe, the OECD countries and China.

4 HIPC (Highly Indebted Poor Countries) initiative; the Doha 'Development Round'; the ESAF (Enhanced Structural Adjustment Facilities); and Sovereign Debt Restructuring Mechanism.

5 Chakravarthi Raghavan, *Recolonization: GATT, the Uruguay Round and the Third World* (London: Zed Books, 1990).

6 Robert Hunter Wade, 'The Rising Inequality of World Income Distribution', *Finance & Development: A Quarterly Magazine of the IMF*, 38, 4 (December 2001) at <www.imf.org/external/pubs/ft/fandd/2001/12/wade.htm>

7 John Cobb and Herman E. Daly, *For the Common Good* (Boston, MA: Beacon Press, 1984, 1997).

8 Tim O'Riordan and James Cameron (eds), *Interpreting the Precautionary Principle* (London: Earthscan, 1994), excerpt at <www.dieoff.org/page31.htm>

9 Note that the UNDP 2000 report encourages a 'multidimensional' perspective on poverty, rather than reducing it to 'monetary' measures. See 'Overcoming Human Poverty: UNDP Poverty Report 2000' at < www.undp.org/povertyreport>; and Barbara Ehrenreich et al. (eds), *Global Women* (New York: Metropolitan Books, 2003).

10 For a travelogue, see Pico Iyer, *The Global Soul* (New York: Vintage, 2000).

11 Michael Wines, 'Yeltsin Agrees to Closer Ties with Belarus', *New York Times*, 26 December 1998, p. A1. The USA has by far the largest share (18 per cent of all votes) and can veto policy decisions, since they require an 85 per cent vote.

12 The third and fifth ministerials collapsed with no agreements, and the progress made at the fourth is widely considered to be rhetorical, rather than substantive.

13 Perhaps the most absurd (and simultaneously well-respected) articulation of this view is Thomas Friedmann's *The Lexus and the Olive Tree* (note the title's Arabization of irrational resistance to globalization!) (New York: Anchor, 2000).

14 In 1996, sub-Saharan Africa paid $2.5 billion more in debt-servicing than it received in new long-term loans and credits. For every dollar sent to the poorest countries in aid, $13 flows back

to lenders in debt service. World Bank figures for 1999 show that $128 million is transferred daily from the sixty-two *most impoverished* countries to wealthy countries: <www.50years.org>

15 For an evaluation of the cooptation of participation and empowerment, see Gary Craig and Marjorie Mayo (eds), *Community Empowerment. A Reader in Participation and Development* (London: Zed Books, 1995); Uma Kothari and Bill Cooke, *Participation: The New Tyranny?* (London: Zed Books, 2001).

16 Amy Chua, *World on Fire: How Exporting Free Market Democracy Breeds Ethnic Hatred and Global Instability* (New York: Anchor, 2003).

17 Vandana Shiva, *Monocultures of the Mind* (London: Zed Books, 1993).

18 Used in South Africa.

19 The original Luddites emerged around 1810 in England, where they resisted the implementation of the knitting frame and other technologies of industrialization (by destroying the equipment). They did not accept the neutrality of technology and argued that its impact on employment, work, community and the quality of the product must govern its implementation. The Luddite movement was quickly and violently repressed by the state.

ONE | **History**

You have arrived, with your anger and your questions. You have arrived, with your hope and your fear. You know that something is wrong, and you know that others know too. You are already part of it and you have been for some time, even if you didn't say so.

You have arrived. Where are you? This new movement already has a long history, but telling it well is a happily impossible project for the reason recognized in the title of the closest such document, *We Are Everywhere* (an astoundingly rich and elaborate brick-shaped book that – if your jeans are fashionably loose – will fit in your pocket).

This is an invitation to the global carnival against capital; because revolt is all the rage, because the struggle for clarity and connection and alternatives is energizing and fun, because finding the power of our communities is something to celebrate. For an invitation, it's hefty: cultural background, glossary, conversation starters, fashion advice ... And, in the next few pages, a rough history. Perhaps you will embrace it as *your* history.

Welcome. Don't be a tourist.

2 Subcomandante Marcos, spokesman for the Zapatista National Liberation Army, in Oaxaca during the 2001 Zapatista Caravan to Mexico City and the halls of congress. Hundreds of thousands of Zapatista supporters met with the caravan during the month-long journey through twelve states (photo by Tim Russo).

2 | It didn't start in Seattle and it didn't stop on 9/11

Telling the history of 'globalization from below' is daunting, because the object of study is what Subcomandante Marcos, former spokesperson for the Ejército Zapatista Liberación Nacional (EZLN), describes as an 'intuition'.[1] Intuition, we are told, is just a mystical word for knowledge – in this case knowledge which is not at all subtle or spiritual in the post-colonial world. As Vandana Shiva pointed out in Seattle, globalization is not a new phenomenon: 'The first globalization was colonialism, and it lasted 500 years. The second globalization was so-called "development", and it lasted 50 years. The third globalization was "free trade" and it only lasted 5 years.' And, since Seattle, we now speak of a fourth globalization, 'people's globalization', which Richard Falk had already theorized as 'globalization from below'.[2]

Rising inequality, unsatisfying experiences with postmodern products, and a storm of what the Marxists call 'contradictions' are reaching, if unevenly, explosive proportions. Argentina combusts, resolving to 'get rid of them all'. London parties with pneumatic drills, digging vegetable gardens in the middle of the cities. India laughs at the World Bank. Safety-suited ghosts go 'midnight gardening' to 'harvest' biotech crops before they can grow. Hysterical apparitions, clinging to life against capital, ‘recognize themselves in one another and get together for some serious analysis at the annual World Social Forum and, more frequently, at regional Social Fora.

Telling the history of the movement is a precarious practice, because it really goes back over five hundred years. For indigenous peoples anywhere, colonialism never ended. Theirs is an uninterrupted struggle against genocide, displacement and cultural invasion.[3] All that has changed is that their struggles now resonate alarmingly with those of privileged people trying to maintain control of their land, labour, livelihood, environment and culture. So while the movement is very, very old, it has entered a new phase in which some genuinely global movements, recognizing themselves in others and others in themselves, are forging not only some notions of solidarity, but a unified voice saying '*ya basta*' (enough!), and articulating detailed visions of 'another world'.

IMF and World Bank Structural Adjustment Programmes (SAPs), beginning in 1980, institutionalized a shift from 'development' practices, systematically imposing foreign control over law and economic policy on postcolonial nations. Throughout the postcolonial period, the former colonizers had influenced and controlled Third World nations through various means (primarily propping up client regimes against nationalist, socialist and democratic movements). SAPs were more bureaucratic, rationalized and irreversible methods of control.

SAPs dismantled many of the accomplishments of postcolonial regimes, reversing the nationalization of industries, cutting anti-poverty programmes, downgrading civil services and revoking land reforms. Their implementation was greeted by 'IMF riots' or 'bread riots' – insurrections including general strikes, massive street protests and the confiscation of food and other basic needs. According to the series of reports called *States of Unrest* put out by the World Development Movement: 'the fiercest critics of IMF and World Bank policies were the people most affected by them ... This [2002] report documents protests in 23 countries ... 76 documented fatalities, and arrests and injuries running into thousands.'[4]

Responding to the devastation of SAPs, the African Council of Churches called in 1990 for the year of Old Testament Jūbilee to forgive African debt. British debt campaigners took notice and started to work with this idea. Similar to liberation theology, the Jubilee movement linked radical political economy with a theologically-founded culture of resistance and demanded relief for 'odious debt' in the Third World.

While US movements splintered into 'identity politics'

during the 1980s, in Europe the politics of the person, of every-day life, retained a class character while also going beyond freedom from material want to demand cultural freedom. The resulting movements built autonomous institutions to meet needs which also confronted commodification and institution-alization. These autonomous movements are well documented by George Katsiaficas in *The Subversion of Politics: European Autonomous Social Movements and the Decolonization of Every-day Life*. Using blockades, occupations and mass actions, they took control of buildings and entire districts for years with a commitment to antifa (antifascism), taking direct action to pro-tect immigrants from racists and immigration police alike.

Ideas of autonomous organization were familiar and well-developed throughout radical European movements. Auto-nomen expressed many of the ideas of anarchism, without being explicitly called anarchist (although many anarchists participated). Infoshops, social centres, squats, street block-ades and property crime against corporations were familiar tactics in Europe by the end of the 1980s. Katsiaficas argues that 'the Autonomen in many countries paralleled one another more than they conformed to mainstream politics or even to countercultural values in their own countries'. When, in 1988, 80,000 people came from across Europe to protest at an IMF meeting in Berlin (explicitly linking IMF policies with the cut-ting of social welfare in Europe and with militarism and im-perialism), 'the initiative of the Autonomen resulted in larger actions, and they were the militant organizers creating a context in which other forms of participation such as signing petitions had meaning'.[5]

In addition to IMF riots in the Third World and autonomia in Europe, there were a number of national and local move-ments during the 1980s which played important roles in the development of globalization from below.

1985 was an auspicious year. The Narmada dam struggles drew together groups which had been fighting dam-related problems in India since the 1970s. In 1988 there were 'mass consultations' and eventually simultaneous actions across the

Narmada Valley which transformed the struggle from a demand for compensation to opposition to the dam itself.[6] These new organizations also began to internationalize the struggle.

Also in 1985 the Movimento dos Trabalhadores Rurais Sem Terra (MST), or Landless Workers' Movement, formalized in Brazil the practice of large-scale land occupations which had been taking place since 1978.[7] Much like the European Auto-nomen, this movement is focused on decommodifying land and establishing autonomous life for a community. Sem Terra operates independently of both church and party politics (even of the Workers' Party, PT). Within ten years or so the MST used a process of militant occupation and then legalization of settle-ments to resettle more than 350,000 families in twenty-three of the twenty-seven Brazilian states. In 1999 alone, 25,099 families occupied land. They also built sixty food cooperatives, inde-pendent education programmes and so forth. The occupations confront the entire system of modernization and urbanization through the collective articulation of underemployed urban workers' desire for autonomy, land and rural community.

Greenpeace London (no connection to Greenpeace Inter-national) in 1985 launched the International Day of Action Against McDonald's, which has been held on 16 October ever since. In 1986 they produced a factsheet, 'What's Wrong with McDonald's? – Everything They Don't Want You to Know'. The leaflet attacked almost all aspects of the corporation's business, accusing it of exploiting children with advertising, promoting an unhealthy diet, exploiting the staff, environmental damage and ill treatment of animals. McDonald's filed a libel suit, but the veracity of the activists' claims triumphed. Throughout the trial, support campaigns battled the company's expensive PR with homemade signs and grassroots organizing.[8]

Another early anti-corporate campaign that influenced the emerging anti-globalization movement was the boycott of Nestlé, on the basis of its deceptive advertising of milk sub-stitutes in the Global South. An international boycott was built in ten First World countries from 1977 to 1984. According to INFACT, one of the organizations that ran the boycott, 'the occasion marked the first time in history that a movement of ordinary people had forced a transnational corporation to deal directly with them at the negotiating table'. The movement also resulted in a World Health Organization (WHO) marketing code for milk substitutes which was implemented through legislation in member countries.

In 1986, Coordination Paysanne Européenne was formed, affirming common interests in family farming, sustainability and solidarity with all farmers rather than competition between them. In 1992, European and Latin American farmers together created an international farmers' organization, the Vía Campesina, which includes small and medium-sized producers, agricultural workers, rural women and indigenous peoples. These new farmers' organizations were innovative in their embrace of solidarity with other farmers' organizations, and their insistence on autonomous and pluralistic actions – separate from all political parties.

In 1990 a first Continental Encounter of Indigenous Peoples was organized in Quito, Ecuador. Delegates from over 200 indigenous nations launched a movement to achieve continental unity. To sustain the process a Continental Coordinating Commission of Indigenous Nations and Organizations (CONIC) was formed at a subsequent meeting in Panama in 1991. According to Harry Cleaver, the unity built was 'not the unity of the political party or trade union – solidified and perpetuated through a central controlling body – but rather a unity of communication and mutual aid among autonomous nations and peoples'.[9] A second Continental Encounter was organized in October 1993 at Temoaya, Mexico. One of the hosting groups at that meeting was the Frente Independiente de Pueblos Indios (FIPI) and one of the groups in FIPI was from San Cristobal, Chiapas – the region from which the Zapatistas would shortly emerge.

In 1991, more than ten years of agitation in India's Narmada Valley led to an unprecedented World Bank investigation of its own project, the Sardar Sarovar dam, which resulted in the pull-out of all Bank monies in 1993, despite nearly $300 million being unrecoverable. By 1997, the struggle had spread to many more dams and the Supreme Court of India had ordered a halt to the construction of Sardar Sarovar. In India, the struggle against modernization gained force.

The next major event took place in 1992 when the indigenous U'wa people in Colombia decided they would not permit Occidental Petroleum to drill in their homeland. It took ten years but in 2002 Occy finally withdrew. This was one of many such struggles which gained intense international attention in the context of an emerging comprehensive case against corporations. Radical environmental organizations embraced the issue, shareholder activism was used, pressure was put on the US Democratic Party for Al Gore's ties to Occidental Petroleum, and massive public and student campaigns pressured the Colombian government.

January 1, 1994, was the day of implementation of the most aggressive Free Trade Agreement (FTA) of the decade, the only one including 'investor rights' and allowing 'investor to state' dispute resolution. On the same day, what has probably been the most important single influence on the anti-globalization movement took form. Emerging from the mountain forest in the poorest state in Mexico, a mysterious army of peasants and indigenous peoples, spouting poetry, took over several towns. The Ejército Zapatista de Liberación Nacional (EZLN) proceeded to establish autonomous zones which have survived even the oppressive presence of half the Mexican military and direct orders from Wall Street[10] to eliminate them. The Zapatistas said, 'They are trying to turn Mexico into a shopping mall' and 'We thought we were up against the state of Mexico, but in reality we were up against the great financial powers.'

Creating an autonomous political space, they ran their own *consultas* (plebiscites) all over Mexico, hosted 'intergalactic Encuentros' in 1996 and 1997,[11] and sent encouraging love-poems to the rest of the world inviting (in a post-identity-politics prophecy) *everyone* to become a Zapatista! The tremendous international solidarity was powerful, but what blunted the force of the military repression was actually resistance from within Mexico from labour unions, peasant federations and the arrival of delegations of indigenous people from all over Latin America organized by FIPI.[12] The Zapatistas marked the new confluence of indigenous and peasant groups, reaching new levels of organizing through developments such as the Latin American Congress of Rural Organizations (CLOC) which met for the first time later in 1994 in Lima Peru.

In the same year, the International Forum on Globalization (IFG) led a renaissance of praxis. It organized dramatic teach-ins at mobilizations of activists,[13] published related texts,[14] and put forward early topical analyses on frontier aspects of globalization, such as the privatization of water. The IFG was thoroughly internationalist and activist, centred on a Global South anti-imperialist perspective, and it united the Global North and South in solidarity on issues of globalization. The organization's goals are twofold: '(1) Expose the multiple effects of economic globalization in order to stimulate debate, and (2) Seek to reverse the globalization process by encouraging ideas and activities which revitalize local economies and communities, and ensure long-term ecological stability.' These eminent scholars, many trained as political economists, implemented a strategic moratorium on the words 'Marx' and 'capitalism' with the result that socialists reviled them and lots of other people listened.

1995 was the year of the creation of the WTO, vigorous French strikes resisting privatization, and the execution of Ken Saro-Wiwa, an activist of the forty-year Ogoni struggle against oil exploitation in Ogoniland. He was executed along with eight other activists by the state of Nigeria. Saro-Wiwa was the first martyr to gain international attention for struggling specifically against corporations. Shell Oil, whose role in the prosecution caused international outrage, was subsequently revealed to be arming and directing the activities of the Nigerian military.[15]

The same year brought the development in London of one of the new tactics of the emerging movement. As the anti-roads movement developed an anti-corporate critique (influenced by the style of the autonomen), the UK government conveniently criminalized rave parties and a combustible political collaboration was formed called Reclaim the Streets, joyfully asserting the primacy of people over the automobile and the state.

In 1996, largely in response to problems of globalization, general strikes rolled through Latin America, but in Ecuador, Brazil and Bolivia, the strikes were for the first time alliances of peasants, indigenous peoples and trade unions. Starting later in the year, South Korean unions held a series of general strikes in protest at a national labour law designed to increase employers' power in the interest of 'competitiveness'. For the first time in Korea, 'democratization' was extended to the economy, and white-collar and other constituents were represented as 'labour'. Farmers and students supported workers battling riot police. By early February, the government had to scrap the proposed changes.[16] Building on the strike wave begun in 1995, two million French workers struck in October 1996 against 'austerity measures' – identical policies of structural adjustment implemented in Europe. In December 1997, French activists formed the first European unemployed union, promoting a new analysis and tactic which quickly spread across Europe.[17]

Starting in July 1997 and continuing through 1998, the economists' promises were returned due to 'insufficient funds' in a wave of collapses throughout the Asian 'dragon' economies, which had sported high levels of growth during the 1980s. The effect on workers, farmers and small businesses was devastating and diverse movements appeared resisting privatization, austerities imposed by the Asian Development Bank and US militarism. In the same year the Fair Labor Organization was established to oversee certification of Fair Trade products.

1998 was the big year in the emergence of the anti-globalization movement. January saw the occupation by 24,000 people of one of the major dams in the Narmada Valley, an escalation of the struggle, which became international and spread to Japan, Germany and the USA in early 1999.[18] February saw the formation of Peoples' Global Action (PGA, having been conceptualized at a Zapatista Encuentro). The 'non-organization' affirmed the development of indigenous forms of resistance to globalization all over the world and put out a 'call to action' for the upcoming WTO meetings in Geneva. Five hundred members, mostly peasant farmers from India, initiated an 'Intercontinental Caravan of Solidarity and Resistance' across Europe, undertaking sixty-three direct actions, including the destruction of biotech seed and crops.[19]

In May, the first 'human chain to break the chains of debt' of 70,000 people ringed the G8 meeting in Birmingham, England. A few days later, on the 16th (m16), fierce protests greeted the second WTO Ministerial in Geneva, held in the United Nations building. The protest of 10,000 people was very large for Switzerland, which prohibited entry to many European protesters. Nevertheless, unemployed people marched from France, and a bicycle and tractor caravan arrived. This was the first 'global day of action' during which simultaneous, diverse protests against the WTO were held in thirty countries on five continents.[20]

In Geneva, the protest made

> the stated intention of crossing the police barriers, entering and stopping the conference. After an open-air press conference with the convenors and a public announcement to the police of the non-violent nature of the action, several hundred people moved calmly and determinedly forward, some even on their knees to emphasize the non-violence [and] more than a thousand persons, gagged and handbound (to symbolize the situation of the people with respect to the global decision makers) marched in silence ... to the Island of Rousseau (author of *The Social Contract*) in the middle of the city to denounce the replacement of social policy by market forces.[21]

US Citizens in Portland, Arcata and Berkeley and Canadians in Toronto and Ottawa participated in m16 (some using Reclaim the Streets' tactics), but the first major direct action blockade of a globalization meeting in North America happened ten days later at the Conférence de Montréal on Globalized Economies, at which the Secretary-General of the OECD was present. This action contributed to the international campaign, particularly strong in Canada, against the Multilateral Agreement on Investments (similar to NAFTA's controversial Chapter 11), which was ultimately scrapped at the OECD when secret negotiations became unfeasible due to unexpected public scrutiny and outcry.[22]

This was also the year in which anti-biotech movements took off across Europe, Latin America and South Asia. These were primarily consumer movements, demanding that restaurants and grocery stores should not sell biotech food, as well as sabotaging seeds and test crops. The Supreme Court of India upheld a ban on the testing of biotech crops while activist farmers heroically torched fields of suspected biotech plants. In January, Dr Arpad Pusztai revealed his research on biotech potatoes' immune-depressing effects and was promptly fired to international outcry (and successful replication of his research). As a result, within a year the seven largest grocery chains in six European countries bowed to public pressure and committed themselves to being 'GM-free'. In the USA, the first few months of 1998 attracted the largest flow of public comment ever received on a proposed national standard, the new Organic Standards Act. This pressure reversed several controversial elements of the corporate-influenced proposal, including the qualification of biotech as organic.

Anti-sweatshop movements which had been developing in North America for nearly a decade took powerful new shape with the formation of United Students Against Sweatshops (USAS) in mid-1998. University students would develop autonomous campus campaigns to demand that university logo gear and sporting equipment were 'sweat-free'.[23]

On 12 August, José Bové and other farmers organized the dismantling of a McDonald's in Millau, France, as a response to the US trade attack on Roquefort as punishment for Europeans' refusal to eat beef grown with hormones. Bové had been involved in the development of the French and European farmers' movement, helping to organize Confédération Paysanne in 1987. In honour of McDonald's, he had created the term '*malbouffe*', a French idiom arousing disgust, literally translated as 'bad food', and he had campaigned against biotech crops. In preparation for the trial, the farmers' union built connections with other social sectors and international activists, ensuring that globalization itself would be on trial. Many expert critics of globalization testified as witnesses and over 100,000 people from Western Europe surrounded the courthouse on 30 June 2000, attended fora and festivities celebrating their new movement of resistance. The international movement's presence at the trial pressured the entire political system: 'A country judge, sitting alone, is not competent to provide the answers to the havoc created by the global market.'[24]

October saw the formation of ATTAC (the International Movement for Democratic Control of Financial Markets and their Institutions) to organize a widespread interest in the Tobin

Tax (James Tobin's proposal for a small tax on international currency transactions).[25] ATTAC went on skilfully to develop that reformist sentiment into a comprehensive political and economic challenge, aiming to 'reconquer space lost by democracy to the sphere of finance, to oppose any new abandonment of national sovereignty on the pretext of the "rights" of investors and merchants, to create a democratic space at the global level. It is simply a question of taking back, together, the future of our world.' ATTAC has chapters in thirty-three countries.

In June 1999, the second 'global carnival of resistance' (j18) was held simultaneously in forty-three countries at the time of the G8 summit in Koln and included a surprising insurrection in London's financial centre. November was a tremendous month, and not only because of the Seattle WTO protests. Earlier in the month, at the Jubilee South–South Summit in Gauteng, South Africa, thirty-five countries gathered to devise a common analysis, vision and strategy regarding debt.

The significance, then, of the 'n30' Seattle protests was not, as is often mis-stated, 'the beginning of a new global movement' – that was already well underway; what it heralded was the entry of US citizens into that movement. Although maximum estimates of 70,000 protesters could hardly compare with ordinary manifestations in the Global South, Seattle was nevertheless significant for the rest of the world. The protest was also special because of the success of the direct action blockade. Using entirely non-violent tactics, protesters locked themselves to one another and sat in the street, preventing all traffic flow, and stood photogenically arm in arm surrounding the convention centre, denying entry to delegates. For a time, police did nothing while bemused delegates sat in the streets talking with protesters. The protest message was clear: the meetings are undemocratic. 'If we can't go in, no one does. Go home!'[26] Some unions compared the action to the Boston Tea Party. Indigenous people issued their own Seattle declaration, stating:

We believe that the whole philosophy underpinning the WTO

Agreements and the principles and policies it promotes contradict our core values, spirituality and worldviews, as well as
our concepts and practices of development, trade and environmental protection ... Indigenous peoples, undoubtedly, are the
ones most adversely affected by globalization and by the WTO
Agreements. However, we believe that it is also us who can
offer viable alternatives to the dominant economic growth,
export-oriented development model. Our sustainable lifestyles
and cultures, traditional knowledge, cosmologies, spirituality, values of collectivity, reciprocity, respect and reverence
for Mother Earth, are crucial in the search for a transformed
society where justice, equity, and sustainability will prevail.

The third 'global day of action' was on! In Geneva, the
untended WTO building was occupied and festooned with
banners reading 'No Commerce, no Organization: Self-
management!' and 'WTO Kills People – Kill the WTO!' Outside
the building, 2,000 farmers and 3,000 city-dwellers converged.
In other cities, coordinated protests targeted the World Bank,
financial centres, biotech companies and US embassies. In
France, 75,000 people took to the streets in eighty different
cities protesting the dictatorship of the markets, McDonald's,
and the WTO. Five thousand French farmers with their live-
stock feasted on regional products under the Eiffel tower, protesting the impact of trade liberalization, while French miners
clashed with police, ransacked a tax office and burned cars.
In Bangalore, India, the campaign 'Monsanto Quit India' was
launched.

2000 began with the indigenous movements of Ecuador
(supported by the military) taking over all three arms of government and declaring their own *parlamentos populares* as the
acting government. The popular uprising was reversed, and
became just one more step in the long struggle for an alternative development. The Cartagena Protocol on BioSafety was
completed in January.[27] During the negotiations, Global South
countries had organized the Like-Minded Group which fought
the US-led Miami Group, demanding national sovereignty in

regulating the entry of genetically modified organisms. While the Like-Minded Group won on most of the text, they lost on the most important paragraph which stated that WTO rulings would take priority over the Protocol, eviscerating both national sovereignty and the precautionary principle.

In February 2000, hundreds of people, mostly belonging to the U'wa and Guahibo peoples, peacefully blockaded roads in U'wa territory. The Colombian military, under pressure from Occidental Petroleum, fired tear-gas from helicopters, forcing protesters including women, children and the elderly into a nearby river. As a result, three children drowned and others were injured. This repression received extraordinary international attention in the context of tear-gas-soaked Seattle.

In April 2000, an insurrection and general strike in Cochabamba demanded the cancellation of a water privatization plan in which the Bolivian government had sold the water to a US corporation, Bechtel. The privatization was the most recent of a series of economic policies already being protested by police, teachers, farmers and students. When the city of Cochabamba refused the water privatization, government troops shot to kill. The government finally revoked the contract with Bechtel.[28] The anti-globalization movement celebrated this event as a major victory and Peoples' Global Action held its next Encuentro in Cochabamba in September 2001.

Also in April, the second major US mobilization was organized at the spring joint meetings of the IMF and World Bank in Washington DC. While stories conflict about the impact of the blockades on the meetings (some claim the meetings went forward without a hitch, other insiders claim that they were in fact seriously disrupted while archived footage was broadcast to deter protesters).

In June, the Soweto Electricity Crisis Committee was formed in response to massive cut-offs of people unable to pay for electricity. The South African state-owned electricity commission was preparing itself for privatization under the post-apartheid government's Igoli 2002 privatization plan – betraying gains won by black South Africans from the apartheid regime in the

Cochabamba Declaration on the Right to Water, January 2001

1. Water belongs to the earth and all species and is sacred to life, therefore, the world's water must be conserved, reclaimed and protected for all future generations and its natural patterns respected.

2. Water is a fundamental human right and a public trust ... therefore, it should not be commodified, privatized or traded for commercial purposes ...

3. Water is best protected by local communities and citizens ... Peoples of the earth are the only vehicle to promote earth democracy and save water.

1980s. The SECC performed reconnections, transformed illegal connections from 'a criminal deed ... into an act of defiance', disconnected politicians' home lines, and went on to remove pre-pay meters and deliver them to politicians' offices.[29] The broader Anti-Privatization Forum was founded in July, embracing issues concerning water, electricity and evictions.

September was busy. On the 11th, World Economic Forum meetings in Melbourne were successfully blockaded Seattle-style by protesters arm-in-arm, and a similar police riot ensued. Then on the 26th, the Prague joint IMF and World Bank meetings were entirely disrupted with the intent of frightening participants from ever attending again. At the meetings the Jubilee movement presented to the Secretary-General of the UN 24 million signatures demanding the cancellation of Third World debt.

In December, another Global South summit on the debt met in Dakar to articulate strategies for resistance to neoliberalism. The Dakar Declaration issued 'demands' on different sectors including Third World social forces, African and Third World heads of state, women's organizations, youth, artists, athletes, African academics, NGOs supporting development, and Northern countries' 'progressive forces'.

> ### The Dakar Declaration for the Total and Unconditional Cancellation of African and Third World Debt, Adopted in Dakar, Senegal, 14 December 2000
>
> Third World debt to the North is at once fraudulent, odious, illegal, immoral, illegitimate, obscene and genocidal; countries of the North owe Third World countries, particularly Africa, a manifold debt: blood debt with slavery; economic debt with colonization, and the looting of human and mineral resources and unequal exchange; ecological debt with the destruction and the looting of its natural resources; social debt (unemployment; mass poverty) and cultural debt (debasing of African civilizations to justify colonization) ... The debt structure and its computation are beyond the debtors' control ... Debt and structural adjustment plans (SAPs) constitute the principal causes for the degradation of health, education, nutrition, food security, the environment and sociocultural values of the African and Third World populations.
>
> *Source*: <www.50years.org/ejn/v4nl/dakar.html>

At the end of January 2001, instead of trying again to sneak into Davos, Switzerland, to protest against the World Economic Forum,[30] social movements gathered in the World Social Forum (WSF) to discuss the alternatives to corporate globalization – 'a symbolic rupture with everything Davos stands for [and] from the South'.[31] Meanwhile, Ecuadorian movements again shut down the country.

In April, the Summit of the Americas met in Quebec City to discuss further the Free Trade Area of the Americas (FTAA/ALCA/ZLÉA), which is intended to extend NAFTA to the thirty-nine states of Latin America. In preparation for the event, Canada erected a huge perimeter fence that was quickly dubbed 'Canada's shame'. Festive trilingual protests flooded the city and a large militant component quickly tore down a portion of the fence. For two days the police soaked an entire neighbourhood with tear-gas, distracting the media from the official events and putting the phrase 'anti-capitalist' into the news media, even in the USA, which is rare.

On 15 June, protests at the EU summit in Gothenburg were greeted by the first use in Sweden since 1931 of live ammunition against protesters. Only a month later, at the G8 meetings in Genoa, Italian police attacked pacifist marches, raided a sleeping place brutally (including lining people up along the walls and beating them) and fatally shot a protester, Carlo Giuliani, the first Global North martyr of the movement. European and Latin American solidarity protests accused Italy of a political assassination. The first photo circulated on the internet of Carlo's murder was 'culture jammed' to show the blood coming out of his head in the shape of Italy, portraying his murder as evidence of the resurgence of fascism in service of global capitalism.

Also in June, well-organized general strikes along with massive and effective occupations and blockades forced the government of Peru to cancel the privatization of the electricity companies. During the strikes and demonstrations, banks and companies which had been privatized and sold were also targeted for attack.[32]

In the first week of September, the South African Anti-Privatization Forum approached the United Nations Durban World Conference Against Racism with the message, 'Simply, we believe that the kinds of neoliberal policies forced upon the South African government by international pressures and by comprador forces within the ruling party's own ranks, are racist.'[33] During the same week, the first World Forum on Food Sovereignty met in Havana, Cuba, asserting: 'They try to deceive the population when they claim that peasant and indigenous farmers and artisanal fisheries are inefficient and unable to meet the growing needs for food production. They use this claim in the attempt to impose widescale, intensive industrial agriculture and fishing.'[34]

Immediately after the events of 9/11, the United States

35

pressured allies to criminalize activists in the guise of coun-ter-terrorism.[35] This had a temporary, chilling effect on some movements in the Global North. Impressive plans for the autumn IMF/World Bank meetings at the end of September in Washington DC were scaled back.

Resisting the chill, a few organizations did still manage to protest at the fourth WTO Ministerial in Doha, Qatar (despite a lack of civil rights there).[36] Anti-globalization forces hailed the meeting location itself as a victory, because the WTO was visibly retreating from democracy. But the chill did not reach the Global South. Beginning in December 2001, Argentinians reacted against IMF policy (ousting a series of presidents will-ing to collaborate with structural adjustment recommenda-tions). The Bolivian insurrection continued to grow.

At the end of January 2002, the World Economic Forum moved its meetings from Davos to New York City, offering 'solidarity' in the form of 'trickle down' spending. Instead, the meetings cost the strapped city millions of dollars for security. This outrage attracted the first post-9/11 protest of the US anti-globalization movement, timidly asserting that 'protest is not terrorism'. Act Now to Stop War & End Racism (ANSWER, which had emerged immediately after 9/11 as the largest convener of anti-war actions, organizing most of the large pacifist marches in the USA, and which was a firm proponent of anti-imperialist analysis) took aim at the WEF's meetings from one side while the direct action anti-globalization component came from the other. Simultaneously, over 51,000 people from 123 countries went to Porto Alegre for the World Social Forum, asserting that 'another world is possible'.[37]

In April, the popular movements of Venezuela refused to permit a coup (widely believed to have been sponsored by the USA) against President Chávez. In August, the first Asian Social Movements meeting was held. Farmers, fisherfolk and workers again affirmed the continuity between issues of global econom-ics and US militarism.

In September, the UN-sponsored corporate-dominated W$$D (World Summit on Sustainable Development), met in

Asian Social Movements Meeting, Bangkok, August 2002

- We demand an end to all US military presence and intervention in Asia – specifically in Afghanistan, Korea, Japan, Philippines and Uzbekistan. We condemn US and British threats to invade Iraq.

- We call for a region-wide campaign to get the IMF, the World Bank and the ADB out of Asia and the Pacific. We demand a complete end to all structural adjustment programmes in any name or form, and an immediate halt to all privatization programmes.

- We resolve to derail the WTO's Fifth Ministerial Meeting in Cancún in September 2003. We will support the development and practice of trade rules that are in the democratic control of the people, promote equality, and strengthen rather than strangle national economies.

- We resolve to support the rights of minority groups, class struggles, and the struggles of all peoples towards self-determination.

Source: <www.focusweb.org/publications/declarations/Statement-of-asian-social-movements-meeting-2002.html>

Johannesburg, where it was thoroughly repudiated by social movements, particularly those of South Africa and India, who exposed the promotion of neoliberal corporate policies under the guise of sustainability, including water privatization and biotechnology.

As the USA geared up for unilateral imperialist war on Iraq, the World Social Forum was organizing fourteen regional and national preparatory fora. The European Social Forum was held in Florence in November 2002. When the anti-globalization convention called for a march against the war, one million persons participated, again showing the close connection between the anti-globalization and anti-imperialist movements.

In 2003, 100,000 people went to Porto Alegre for the annual World Social Forum, where informed pundits such as Noam Chomsky issued surprisingly optimistic statements about the 'gloomy' mood of global capitalists faced with anti-imperialist insurrections all over the world. In 2005, over 200,000 people participated in the WSF. Regional fora proliferate, each surrounded by alter-fora, youth and indigenous encampments.

On the heels of the WSF, Bolivian movements faced with a new tax imposed as structural adjustment burned the banks, recruited the police to the side of the people, organized a general strike and called for the resignation of the president. The noxious policy was revoked within days. And in October the movements forced the resignation of yet another president, requiring the new one to renationalize oil and gas within ninety days, as well as revoke the coca eradication programme.

The coordinated international protests against the Iraq War on 15 February 2003 drew on the tactic of global days of action first realized by the fledgling anti-globalization movement in 1998. This day forcefully communicated a clear anti-imperialist message with solidarity among at least 14 million persons internationally. The fact that tiny protests were held in remote locations on this day marks the emergence of a truly global movement.

In early 2005, we find generation of 'another world' on a continental scale as Bolivia's struggle against privatization expands to the point that the President gave up. Venezuela ferociously deepens its democratization, Uruguay elects its first socialist in decades, and militant resistance to globalization grows in Ecuador, Guatemala, Brazil and Argentina.

This history, while hardly a comprehensive one, maps the emergence and convergence of movement hallmarks: diversity, solidarity, creativity, autonomy, direct action and the creation of spaces of participatory democracy.[38]

Resources

Notes from Nowhere (ed.), *We Are Everywhere: The Irresistible Rise of Global Anti-capitalism* (London: Verso, 2003).

John Ross, *The War Against Oblivion: Zapatista Chronicles 1994-2000* (Monroe, ME: Common Courage Press, 2000).

Al Gedicks and Roger Moody, *Resource Rebels* (Boston, MA: South End Press, 2001).

John Vidal, *McLibel: Burger Culture on Trial* (New York: New Press, 1998).

Tom Mertes (ed.), *A Movement of Movements: Is Another World Really Possible?* (London: Verso, 2004).

David McNally, *Another World is Possible: Globalization and Anti-capitalism* (Winnipeg: Arbeiter Ring, 2002).

Eddie Yuen et al., *Confronting Capitalism: Dispatches from a Global Movement* (Brooklyn, NY: Soft Skull Press, 2004).

David Bacon, *The Children of NAFTA: Labor Wars on the U.S./Mexico Border* (Berkeley: University of California Press, 2004).

Notes

1 *Zapatista!*, Big Noise Films, 1998. <www.bignoisefilms.com>

2 Richard Falk, 'The Making of Global Citizenship', pp. 39–50 in J. Brecher, J. B. Childs and J. Cutler (eds), *Global Visions: Beyond the New World Order* (Boston, MA: South End Press, 1993).

3 See Al Gedicks and Roger Moody, *Resource Rebels: Native Challenges to Mining and Oil Corporations* (Boston, MA: South End Press, 2001).

4 World Development Movement <www.wdm.org.uk> See also Susan Eckstein (ed.), *Power and Popular Protest: Latin American Social Movements* (Berkeley: University of California Press, 2001).

5 George Katsiaficas, *The Subversion of Politics: European Autonomous Social Movements and the Decolonization of Everyday Life* (New Jersey: Humanities Press, 1997), pp. 265, 131.

6 Chittaroopa Palit, 'Monsoon Risings: Mega-Dam Resistance in the Narmada Valley' (May 2003), pp. 71–93 in Tom Mertes (ed.), *A Movement of Movements: Is Another World Really Possible?* (London: Verso, 2004).

7 João Pedro Stedile, 'Brazil's Landless Battalions: The Sem Terra Movement' (May 2002), pp. 17–48 in Mertes (ed.), *A Movement of Movements*.

8 See <www.mcspotlight.org/case>

9 Harry Cleaver, 'The Chiapas Uprising in the New World Order', Summer 1994. Originally for RIFF-RAFF, revisions in *Common Sense*, Edinburgh, 15 (April 1994); *Canadian Dimension*,

Winnipeg, 28, 3 (May–June 1994): 36–9; *Studies in Political Economy*, Toronto, 44 (Summer 1994); and elsewhere. <www.eco. utexas.edu/faculty/Cleaver/chiapasuprising.html>

10 <www.eco.utexas.edu/faculty/Cleaver/chiapas95.html>

11 The 1997 Encuentro, held in Spain, is credited with gener- ating three crucial new movement formations: Peoples' Global Action, a coordinated international campaign against the WTO, and what was to become Indymedia (Notes from Nowhere [ed.], *We Are Everywhere: The Irresistible Rise of Global Anticapitalism* [London: Verso, 2003], pp. 74, 96).

12 Cleaver, 'The Chiapas Uprising'.

13 Knowing in advance the significance of the Seattle protests, the IFG rented the Seattle Symphony Hall for a three-day teach-in.

14 Edward Goldsmith and Jerry Mander (eds), *The Case Against the Global Economy and for a Turn Toward the Local* (London: Kogan Page, 2001). John Cavanagh, Jerry Mander et al., *Alternatives to Economic Globalization: A Better World is Possible* (San Francisco, CA: Berrett-Koehler, 2002).

15 The executed activists were convicted of murder of four Ogoni leaders. Amnesty International and other groups asserted these charges were false and that the accused were political prisoners. The cases were heard by the Federal Military Govern- ment (a Civil Disturbances Special Tribunal), and appeals were not allowed as guaranteed under Nigeria's constitution and the African Charter for Human and Peoples' Rights, to which Nigeria is a signatory. See *Amnesty International Index*, 'Nigeria: Amnesty International Condemns Execution of Ken Saro-Wiwa and Eight Others', AFR 44/31/95, 10 November 1995. Also Karen McGregor in *Durban Independent* (London), 19 September 2000 at </www. ratical.org/corporations/ShellNigeria.html> Greenpeace archive at <www.archive.greenpeace.org/comms/ken>

16 But when the financial crisis hit South Korea a few months later, nearly identical reforms were promptly passed.

17 Christine Daniel, 'Widespread Protests by Unemployed People: Towards a New Form of Social Movement?', Institut de Recherches Economiques et Sociales, 28 January 1998 <www.eiro. eurofound.ie/1998/01/feature/FR9801189F.html>

18 This dam, the Maheshwar, was finally defeated in 2002. After a five-year stay of construction ordered by the Supreme Court of India, the Sardar Sarovar dam was restarted in 2000.

19 Katherine Ainger, 'Life is Not Business: The Interconti-nental Caravan', pp. 160–70 in News from Nowhere (ed.), *We are Everywhere*.

20 Peoples' Global Action events archive at <www.agp.org>

21 Ibid.

22 MAI was later reintroduced into the WTO as TRIMs (Trade Related Investment Measures).

23 USAS was an important player in the development of the Workers' Rights Consortium in 2000, which demanded independ-ent monitoring in parallel to the Fair Labor Association.

24 José Bové and François Dufour with Gilles Luneau, *The World is not for Sale: Farmers Against Junk Food*, trans. Anna de Casparis (London: Verso, 2002), p. 183.

25 See <www.tobintax.org.uk>

26 Protester in Whispered Media, *Shut Em Down!* (video) at <www.whisperedmedia.org>

27 <www.biodiv.org/default.aspx>

28 In May 2000 Bechtel filed a legal demand for $40 million against the Bolivian people – compensation for its lost opportu-nity to make future profits. The suit was filed through the Inter-national Court for the Settlement of Investment Disputes of the World Bank. Such 'investor rights' to be free of 'expropriation of investor assets' are fully protected in Chapter 11 of NAFTA and the TRIMs agreement in the WTO – formerly the MAI in the OECD.

29 Trevor Ngwane, 'Sparks in the Township' (July 2003), pp. 111–34 in Mertes (ed.), *A Movement of Movements*.

30 The World Economic Forum has held annual members-only retreats for the chief executives of the world's 'foremost corporations' since 1971. The WEF functions as an agenda-setting body with increasingly direct influence over elected policy-makers. In 1982, an 'informal meeting' of seventeen trade ministers, hosted by the WEF, launched the Uruguay Round of GATT negotiations which led to the formation of the WTO. The WEF also takes credit for brokering peace agreements in South Africa, Israel and Greece, revealing distinct corporate influence over those historic events (<www.weforum.org/'History and Achievements'>).

31 Bernard Cassen, 'Inventing ATTAC' (January 2003), pp. 152–74 in Mertes (ed.), *A Movement of Movements*.

32 Jordi Martorell, 'Peru – Mass Uprising Defeats Privatisation Plans', *In Defense of Marxism*, 24 June 2002 at <www.marxist.com>

33 Trevor Ngwane, 'South African Movement, 25 August, 2001', at <www.nadir.org/nadir/initiativ/agp/free/imf/africa/0825movement.htm>

34 'Final Declaration of the World Forum on Food Sovereignty', Havana, Cuba, 7 September 2001.

35 Leo Panitch, 'Whose Violence? Imperial State Security and the Global Justice Movement', *Socialist Project*, Contributions to Socialism Pamphlet Series no. 2, November 2004, at <www.socialistproject.ca>

36 'After the Seattle demonstrations, Qatar was the only WTO Member State willing to host the following Ministerial. In Qatar, freedom of assembly and association, and of demonstrating do not exist. Several NGOs, among which was Human Rights Watch, pointed out how strange and significant it was to hold the WTO Ministerial in one of the few countries which did not ratify the UN International Covenant on civil and political rights' (*La Lettre*, no. 320/2, November 2001, Fédération Internationale des Ligues des Droits de l'Homme, Paris).

37 <www.forumsocialmundial.org.br/home.asp>

38 Notes from Nowhere (ed.), *We are Everywhere*, p. 506.

TWO | **Manifestos**

We do know what we are for

No action happens without many hours of meetings. Together we review the reasons why we have come together. People are angry. If it is a democratic meeting, it can take a long time to hear from everyone, but that means that many details and analyses have been reviewed.

The meetings also take a long time because it's often necessary to debate several alternatives to the current situation before taking action, because people need to act knowing that we share a vision. Then people sometimes disagree about which actions will be most effective.

By the time the meetings have finished and the plan is in place, participants have a new confidence in the identification of our enemies, in the wisdom and skills of our colleagues, and in the new world which we are about to take great risks to bring into being.

Not wanting to bore journalists and pundits with our long meetings, we invite them to see only the action.

We invite everyone to our many seminars. We put a lot of energy into these and other forms of dialogue with our neighbours. We make sure there are many opportunities to learn why we are fighting so hard, how we analyse the world, and our ideas for how it could be better.

In between the times of most intense struggle, we often travel long distances to meet with other activists and groups. At these exciting multilingual meetings we make sure that our analyses are comprehensive enough, we develop sympathy with struggles far away, we share new strategies for action, and we work to develop consensus.

After these meetings, we issue manifestos and declarations for those who could not make it. (These are short and to the point because we need to translate them into so many languages.)

It's astonishing that our diverse struggles, sustained by an array of cultures, buffeted by devastating assaults, have agreed on so much. Equally astonishing is the fact that condescending commentators often ignore the intelligence, collectivity and even the very existence of our manifestos.

3 upper: II Fórum Social Mundial, Porto
Alegre, Brazil, 31 January–5 February
2002 (photo by Leonardo Melgarejo for
Movimento dos Trabalhadores Rurais
Sem Terra – Brazil).   lower: People
from popular organizations throughout
Central America and Mexico met in
the Vth Mesoamerican Forum in San
Salvador to discuss how to strengthen
movements for social change within the
region, July 2004 (photo by Tim Russo)

3 | Participatory democracy: the World Social Forum

The anti-globalization movement has fostered the development of what has the potential to become the most sophisticated and inclusive democratic process undertaken in human history. The World Social Forum (WSF) was initiated in 2001 as a counterpoint to the meetings of the elite World Economic Forum (WEF).

The World Social Forum declares that 'another world is possible' and supports a collaborative process of 'seeking and building alternatives'.[1] There are now regional fora all over the world. The WSF is a 'permanent process' for groups and movements 'opposed to neoliberalism and to domination of the world by capital and any form of imperialism, and ... committed to building a global society of fruitful relationships among human beings and between humans and the Earth'.

The WSF Charter of Principles states that party representatives and military organizations are not permitted to participate in the Forum and that the WSF will oppose 'all totalitarian as well as reductionist views of economy, development and history' as well as 'the use of violence as a means of social control by the state'. This also means that armed resistance movements are controversially excluded.

Participants in the WSF have achieved confident consensus on an exceedingly radical programme, including: immediate repudiation of Third World debt; reparations for slavery; either radical reform or total dismantlement of the IMF, World Bank and WTO; unconditional autonomy of indigenous people; food sovereignty; land reform; and denunciation of direct and proxy imperialism in Palestine, Iraq and elsewhere. The tradition of universalized human rights is understood to be infected with 'westernization and cultural homogeneity' which is the source of many global problems.[2]

Among the many economic alternatives explored at the WSF is 'solidarity-based economics', an attempt to unite livelihood and other small enterprises with participatory democratic practices to ensure both economic security and human-centred development. Other proposals include the rejection of First World norms of standards of living as merely a '*style* of well-being'. Such 'styles' that 'cannot be democratized must not continue to exist, since they destroy the planet on which we all depend for life'.[3] The 'right to the city' protects public services, land, housing, sanitation, livelihood, urban ecology, democracy and urban mobility from the forces which seek to transform cities into spaces of 'passive individual enjoyment and the interests of real-estate capital'.[4]

The WSF framework envisions social movements as the leadership of the process of building another world in a 'movement of movements', which should strive to maintain independence from states, parties and institutions 'despite the presence of professionals who are sympathetic'.[5]

Reinventing democracy

Many anti-globalization movements avoid association with political parties, usually because movements' power has so often been coopted by parties in ways which distorted their agendas. Instead of working with these structures, movements are creating their own methods of building power and making decisions. These include new conceptions of representative democracy ('govern obeying'), widespread use of direct democracy, new sorts of institutions and honouring individual voices and expressions.

We do not want Western money, technologies or 'experts' to impose their development model on us. We refuse to be used as political tools to ask the elites for reforms that we never demanded. We only want to organize our strength and combine it with the strength of other movements in the North and the South in order to regain control over our lives. We are not working for a place at the global table of negotiations, nor for a bloody revolution; we are just working on the long-term process of construction of a different world.[6]

Democracy, participation and autonomy are understood not only as the alternatives to cooptation, reforms and vanguards but as the active defence against them. Discussing the struggles against the Narmada dams, Chittaroopa Palit explains that the movement's slogans were themselves an indication that the movement was participatory, because a vanguardist movement could not promise that 'nobody will move, the dam will not be built' or 'we will drown, but we will not move'.[7] Such commitments depend on a meaningful and participatory political process.

At the World Social Forum, participatory democracy means that, aside from publicizing the major points of consensus, there is no pressure to reach agreement. Participatory democracy is an inclusive space in which to share analyses and methods and to build solidarity from the ground up, without pressure to conform.

Redefining progress

Long before comprehensive analyses of globalization and recolonization were even available, the 'different world' was already being formed. In many contexts (even occasionally under the auspices of international development agencies), people and communities have worked to apply traditional and modern technologies to create ecological and just solutions to community problems. These experiments are particularly advanced in the arena of sustainable development, including not only agriculture, energy technologies and settlement design but also social institutions such as education, childcare, decision-making, multiculturalism and gender equity.

While it is important to keep in mind that the concept of sustainability is rapidly being coopted by corporations and institutions,[8] it is also easy to distinguish between the grassroots and coopted versions. One thing that has been absolutely consistent in grassroots conceptions of sustainability, whether articulated from the Global South or North, has been that economic growth is a primary cause of unsustainability. In contrast, corporate versions of sustainability emphasize 'sustainable growth', an oxymoron. Coopted versions of sustainability tend to position industry and corporations as partners or stakeholders in achieving environmental goals. In grassroots discourse, unsustainable production systems are seen as illegitimate (they do not deserve to be partners and they have no rights as 'stakeholders') not only because they are ecologically suicidal, but also because sustainable development practitioners know that there are sustainable alternatives to any needed industrial products.

Sustainability activists advocate small-scale economies where basic items are produced as close as possible to where they are consumed, where people eat seasonally-appropriate foods, produce energy and dispose of 'waste' in decentralized ways, choose technologies that require minimal inputs and are easily repaired, and minimize consumption of imported and wasteful goods. Sustainable economies are more secure from external economic fluctuations because they are 'highly self-sufficient and integrated, with a minimum of importing and transporting into the area'.[9] Food, fuel, fibre and animal fodder can all be produced sustainably in any part of the world.

Endogenous projects in communities everywhere affirm the possibility of grassroots solutions to all kinds of community problems and needs. While incomplete and imperfect, experiments with Fair Trade, food policy councils, self-housing associations, worker-owned cooperatives, neighbourhood assemblies and decentralized energy production and water harvesting,[10] show viability in generating the social and scientific technologies that will ensure dignified lives for all.

While these experiments have been fruitful, the movements' confidence that another world is possible is rooted in the recuperation from centuries of ridicule of the social and economic methods of indigenous peoples. Hundreds of thousands of distinct peoples lived for millennia, providing for their own material, spiritual, social and political needs. Those who survived colonialism are now continuing a complex process of agentic creolization, despite conditions of seductive cultural invasion, genocidal state-corporate land grabs and biopiracy.

Diverse communities spent thousands of years using the scientific method in agriculture, medicine and ecosystem management.[11] They also refined economic, political, social and educational systems. These advanced traditions, developed in societies in which the market (to the extent it existed) was subordinate to social criteria, are now posed as 'alternatives' by movements which dare to redefine progress as something other than surrendering history, culture and life to business. Survivors of postmodern capitalism are embracing these traditions as methods of achieving their most sophisticated aspirations for sustainable, accountable, diverse and engaged social life.

Resources

World Social Forum: <www.forumsocialmundial.org.br>

PGA WSF pages: <www.nadir.org/nadir/initiativ/agp/free/wsf>

William Fisher and Thomas Ponniah (eds), *Another World is Possible: Popular Alternatives to Globalization at the World Social Forum* (London: Zed Books, 2003), p. 193.

Sustainable technology: Appropriate Technology Library: <www.villageearth.org>

Earthscan Publications: <www.earthscan.co.uk>

Notes

1 WSF 'Charter of Principles', 2002 <www.forumsocial mundial.org.br>

2 For discussions of improvements to the framework of human rights, see Abdullahi A. An-Na'im (ed.), *Human Rights in Cross-Cultural Perspectives: A Quest for Consensus* (Pittsburgh, PA: University of Pennsylvania Press, 1991).

3 William Fisher and Thomas Ponniah (eds), *Another World is Possible: Popular Alternatives to Globalization at the World Social Forum* (London: Zed Books, 2003), pp. 6, 127 (emphasis added).

4. Ibid., p. 174.

5 Ibid., p. 177.

6 Karnataka State Farmers Association of India, 18 June 1999, in Notes from Nowhere (ed.), *We are Everywhere: The Irresistible Rise of Global Anticapitalism* (London: Verso, 2003), p. 160.

7 Chittaroopa Palit, 'Monsoon Risings: Mega-Dam Resistance in the Narmada Valley' (May 2003), pp. 71–93 in Mertes (ed.), *A Movement of Movements: Is Another World Really Possible?* (London: Verso, 2004), p. 89.

8 The increasingly egregious cooptation included the UN's World Summit for Sustainable Development which met in Johannesburg, South Africa, in September 2002. It was greeted by militant protests.

9 F. E. Trainer, 'Reconstructing Radical Development Theory', *Alternatives*, 14, 4 (October 1989), pp. 481–515.

10 Water scarcity in 9,000 villages could be solved through these methods for a total of Rs. 90 billion instead of the Rs. 200 billion slated for the Sardar Sarovar dam. Palit, 'Monsoon Risings'.

11 Pharmaceutical and agro-chemical companies are currently attempting to patent some of this science in a process described as 'biopiracy'.

4 | Don't owe! won't pay! Drop the debt

Total and unconditional debt cancellation for poor countries is increasingly understood to be the most basic building block of international social justice and poverty alleviation. Poor countries are devoting obscene portions of their national economies to debt-servicing, often for debts which in no way benefited the national economy or the poor.

On top of the excessive payments, the structural adjustment programmes implemented by the World Bank and the International Monetary Fund, professing to assist countries in managing payments, effectively liquidate the economy. Not only do these programmes auction off natural and economic resources, they also place an inordinate burden on the poorest, who pay debt service through unaffordable user fees for health, education, water and energy, whose livelihood resources are destroyed or privatized, who suffer increasingly exploitative working conditions, and who pay more for basic goods with each currency devaluation.

'IMF riots' are the most direct response to implementation of structural adjustment.[1] International networks have been fighting since the early 1990s to expose aspects of the debt regime and pressure the debt-holders to 'drop the debt'. In the Global North, these campaigns have emphasized the cuts to healthcare and education mandated by structural adjustment. Debt cancellation would free money now spent on debt service to pay for basic programmes. In the Global South, movements reject the obligation to pay debts which lack credibility and whose only function has been to resurrect the power relations of colonialism.

Still nascent is the threat of debtors' cartels which would collectively refuse or renegotiate debts.[2] Cartels, accompanied by regional trading blocs, could aid the transition of defaulting

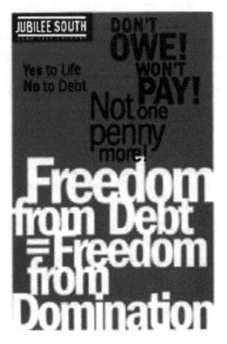

4 Jubilee South poster, c. 1999

countries to independence even in the face of predictable capital and military strikes.

In just fifteen years, drop the debt campaigns have been remarkably successful. International financial institutions (World Bank, IMF and others) have undertaken major initiatives which present the appearance of providing debt relief. These programmes (HIPC, ESAF, etc.) are quantitatively inadequate, make arbitrary and unsupportable distinctions between poor countries, and require continued structural adjustment enforcement as a condition of debt reduction.

Unfazed by cooptation, the international movement has strengthened the demand for 100 per cent debt cancellation. The ranks of critics swell with former debt administrators and international development professionals, who assist in revealing the machinations of the debt regimes. Pressure on the G8 actually to cancel the debt has grown steadily, and by

---

South–South Summit Declaration, 'Towards a Debt-Free Millennium', Gauteng, South Africa, 18–21 November 1999

The External Debt of countries of the South is illegitimate and immoral. It has been paid many times over ... We thus reject the continued plunder of the South by way of debt payments. Peoples and countries of the South are in fact creditors of an enormous historical, social, and ecological debt. This debt must be repaid in order to make possible a 'New Beginning'. In the spirit of Jubilee, we demand restitution of what has been taken unjustly from us, and reparations for the damage wrought ... Debt is essentially an ideological and political instrument for the exploitation and control of our peoples, resources, and countries by those corporations, countries, and institutions that concentrate wealth and power in the global capitalist system.

Don't owe! won't pay!

October 2004 the G7 was only wrangling the details. Actual cancellation is now expected.[3] Campaign groups are working to expand the list of qualified 'poor' countries and to ensure that no 'conditions' will be attached.

Resources

Jubilee South: <www.jubileesouth.org>

Jubilee research: <www.Jubilee2000uk.org>

Debt links: <www.debtlinks.org>

KAIROS Analysis of Debt Relief Initiatives <www.kairoscanada. org/e/economic/debt>

Notes

1 World Development Movement <www.wdm.org.uk> See also Susan Eckstein (ed.), *Power and Popular Protest: Latin American Social Movements* (Berkeley: University of California Press, 2001).

2 Jeremy Brecher, Tim Costello, and Brendan Smith, 'Debtors of the World, Unite', *International Socialist* (August–September 2001). Online at <www.portoalegre2003.org>

3 Emad Mekay, 'No Relief for the Poor', *Inter Press Service*, 2 October 2004. Paul Blustein, 'Debt Relief Plan Eludes IMF Group: Issue Likely to be Resolved Next Year', *Washington Post*, 3 October 2004.

5 | Food sovereignty: farmers need access to local, not global, markets

Food sovereignty is a concept introduced in 1996 by Vía Campesina, the largest of many international farmers' associations. Food sovereignty insists that 'hunger is not a problem of means, but of rights'.[1] These rights include that 'every people, no matter how small, has the right to produce their own food'[2] and 'the right of consumers to be able to decide what they consume, and how and by whom it is produced'.[3] Food sovereignty insists on 'agriculture whose central concern is human beings'[4] and recognizes the central roles of women and indigenous peoples in food production.

In the process of developing international solidarity, Vía Campesina has discovered that family farmers in the Global South and in the North do not need access to global markets. They need access to their *local* markets. As a result, farmers in different countries do not need to compete with one another. 'Only the surplus should be traded, and that only bilaterally.'[8] Trade is beneficial to share 'with other regions specific products which make up diversity on our planet'.[9]

In order to achieve food sovereignty, the most important step is to protect farmers against 'dumping' (imports that undermine the price of local products). The only beneficiaries of dumping are transnational companies. Export companies' interests represented in the agriculture agreements of the WTO and other FTAs cannot be said to represent farmers, as the companies account for only 10 per cent of global food production. 'Access to international markets is not a solution for farmers. The first problem for farmers is a lack of access to their own local market' because of dumping.[5]

International FTAs perversely allow major agriculture exporters to continue subsidizing large producers in myriad ways while outlawing any subsidies to domestic production

5 Durbar Square, Kathmandu, Nepal, November, 1986 (photo copyright Jerry Riley, Toronto, Canada <jerry@colourlab. com>)

and protections of small producers. Dumping is protected, agriculture and rural economies in the Global South are incapacitated and nations become dependent on imported food. The resulting exodus of the rural poor provides cheap labour for foreign manufacture invited in by increasingly desperate governments – and the jobs do not pay enough for food.

Food sovereignty requires governments to orient agricultural policy in support of family farmers and to protect the 'access of peasants and landless people to land, water, seeds, and credit. Hence the need for land reforms, for fighting against [biotechnology], for free access to seeds, and for safeguarding water as a public good to be sustainably distributed.' Land reform, as conceptualized within food sovereignty, goes beyond better distribution of private property to confirm farmers as 'guardians of the land'.[6]

National trade policy must 'prioritize local and regional production' for domestic use, rather than orienting agricultural policy towards exports. Public financial support for farmers is essential to ensure that overproduction does not undermine prices, to 'fulfill other public interests that can differ according to countries and their cultural traditions', and to support sustainable agriculture, but not to facilitate 'export at low prices' (dumping).

International food policy must respect these national priorities and seek, particularly in addressing crises, not to undermine local production. Currently, food aid programmes authorize what amounts to dumping, undermining prices and bankrupting farmers in crisis areas. For Northern exporters, the outcome of Global South famines is profitable long-term dependence.

Food sovereignty also asserts that national governments are obligated to feed people, that access to food should not be a form of assistance, and that food cannot be used as a weapon.

Resources

Vía Campesina: <www.viacampesina.org>

People's Food Sovereignty: <www.peoplesfoodsovereignty.org>

Food First: <www.foodfirst.org>

Frances Moore Lappé, Joseph Collins and Peter Rosset with Luis Esparza, *World Hunger: 12 Myths*, 2nd edn (Oakland, CA: Grove/Atlantic, Food First Books, 1998).

José Bové and François Dufour with Gilles Luneau (trans. Anna de Casparis), *The World is not for Sale: Farmers Against Junk Food* (London: Verso, 2002).

Notes

1 NGO/CSO Forum for Food Sovereignty, parallel with the 2002 World Food Summit, Rome, 8–13 June 2002.

2 João Pedro Stedile, 'Brazil's Landless Battalions: The Sem Terra Movement' (May 2002), pp. 17–48 in Tom Mertes (ed.), *A Movement of Movements: Is Another World Really Possible?* (London: Verso, 2004), p. 43.

3 'Declaration of Dakar: For Mutually Supportive Agricultural and Trade Policies', 21 May 2003.

4 'Declaration of the World Forum on Food Sovereignty', Havana, Cuba, September 2001.

5 Vía Campesina, 'What is Food Sovereignty?' 15 January 2003 at <www.viacampesina.org>

6 Stedile, 'Brazil's Landless Battalions'.

7 Vía Campesina, 'What is Food Sovereignty?'

8 Stedile, 'Brazil's Landless Battalions'.

9 Vía Campesina, 'What is Food Sovereignty?'

6 | Reclaim the commons: no patents on life!

Scientists, farmers and scholars from the Global South have developed a strong consensus on the dangers of biotechnology (particularly of genetically engineered seed) and the violence of biopatenting (the privatization of biodiversity).[1]

Agroindustrial and pharmaceutical companies insist that biopatenting (privatization) is necessary to mobilize the profit motive to 'feed the world' and 'cure disease' through biotechnology. They argue that some environmental and health risk is unavoidable if we are committed to 'feeding the world' and 'curing disease'. The reality is that they are rushing to market unnecessary products and doing so without adequate testing and protection of biodiversity. They are using FTAs to eviscerate the 'precautionary principle' and establish 'timeliness' restrictions on regulation, asserting their 'right' to commercialize products without proper testing or scientific oversight.

While promising to alleviate hunger and disease, these corporations are destabilizing farmers' access to seed and abandoning basic medicine, such as antibiotics research. Pharmaceutical companies have severely cut their antibacterial research programmes, because curing disease is not as profitable as depression and sexual function drugs.[2] Meanwhile, the rapid commercialization of biotechnology threatens to obliterate all alternatives through genetic contamination of traditional and wild varieties. This frightening possibility is the best-case scenario from the point of view of companies who would then be able to monopolize the provision of food and medicine.

The cure for these problems, from the perspective of the social movements engaging them, is to forbid patents on life.[3] Patents, and the super-profits they facilitate, are distorting medical and agricultural science, engineering and regulations

6 'We Will Drown but We Will not Move'
Satyagraha of 21 September 1999, Domkhedi,
Narmada Valley (photo by Harikrishna
Katragadda courtesy of Friends of River
Narmada)

on marketing and release. Outlawing patents on life is the necessary first step towards ensuring that biodiversity, information, research agendas and regulatory mechanisms stay in public control.

Movements concerned with these issues have completed major international legal projects, including the Convention on Biodiversity (1992) and the Cartagena Protocol on Biosafety (2000), intended to protect biodiversity from biotechnology. Inside the WTO, the African Group, supported by a cluster of Asian organizations,[4] made a proposal in 2003 within the intellectual property agreements (TRIPS) which would allow countries to prohibit the patenting of life.[5]

In the meantime, without waiting for international law, activists take direct action. Thousands of local groups uproot biotech crops to prevent genetic pollution, confront biotech companies, prohibit or refuse biotech foods and defend biodiversity.

Half of the world's remaining biodiversity is in the protection of indigenous peoples. Biopatenting depends on their scientific knowledge. In December of 2001, shamans from twenty indigenous peoples in the Amazon region met to frame a position on indigenous knowledge. They asserted that knowledge about both the sustainable management of these resources and their use is inseparable from indigenous 'identities, laws, institutions, value systems and our cosmological vision'. Given the unwillingness of states to protect indigenous peoples' rights, the letter of São Luís do Maranhão suggests the establishment of a moratorium on indigenous cooperation with commercial exploration of traditional knowledge.

The framework 'No Patents on Life' is part of a larger movement to 'reclaim the commons'. Commons are protected by thousands of diverse 'commons regimes', communal management which defines equitable access for direct uncommodified use by the community and restrains overuse. From 1100–1700, with the assistance of state resources including laws called Acts of Enclosure, British elites appropriated forests, forages and collective agricultural lands from commons use, handily

63

**São Luís do Maranhão Letter,
6 December 2001**

14. We propose to the government that it recognize traditional knowledge as science, giving it a equivalent status in relation to western scientific knowledge, establishing a science and technology policy which recognizes the importance of traditional knowledge.

15. We propose the adoption of a universal means of legally protecting traditional knowledge, an alternative system, a sui generis system, distinct from other laws protecting intellectual property rights which also addresses the following issues: the recognition of indigenous territories and their consequent demarcation; the recognition of the collective ownership of traditional knowledge; local indigenous communities' right to deny access to traditional knowledge and to genetic resources found in their territories; the recognition of indigenous peoples' traditional forms of social organization; the inclusion of the principle of prior informed consent and a clear willingness to respect the participation of indigenous peoples in the equitable sharing of the benefits arising from the use of these resources and knowledge and which permits the continuity of the free exchange between indigenous peoples of their resources and traditional knowledge.

Source: <www.grain.org/bio-ipr/?id=273#>

creating at once both private land and desperate 'free' labour. (When separated from their commons subsistence resources, people must then depend on selling their labour.) This process foreshadowed colonial methods. While many commons regimes have been stolen or weakened by market pressures to commodify resources for external sale, many commons, such as farmers' marketplaces, are still governed traditionally, by their users.

The modern movement to 'reclaim the commons' includes

'reclaim the commons' includes refusal to move for dams and other collective collective land claims, such as those established by the Movimento dos Trabalhadores Rurais in Brazil. Reclaim the commons is also a framework for managing biodiversity, seeds, indigenous knowledge, forests, rivers and fisheries. Understanding these resources as an unownable heritage, 'reclaim the commons' urges resistance to privatization of any kind. Asserting these resources as commons protects access for small producers and the poor who will be locked out of a market-based system. The commons framework is sometimes extended to other resources under threat of privatization, such as energy, education, the airwaves, the internet and other civic spaces.

No commons can be conceptualized independently of its commons regime, which is the social mechanism that protects both the resource and people's access to it. In 2002, participants in the World Social Forum drafted a Treaty to Share the Genetic Commons, which asserts genetic resources as commons property that cannot be bought and sold, and also a treaty initiative on the water commons, which protects access to water for all human beings. Commenting on the growing rhetoric of 'global commons', Vandana Shiva warns: 'These treaties will have democratic power and substance to the extent they strengthen local community rights at the global level. Global commons not based on local commons is an ecologically and democratically fraudulent category.'[6]

Resources

Research Foundation for Science, Technology and Ecology: <www.vshiva.net>

The Ecologist magazine, *Whose Common Future?: Reclaiming the Commons* (Gabriola Island, BC, Canada: New Society, 1993).

Convention on Biodiversity: <www.biodiv.org>

Biosafety Protocol: <www.biodiv.org/biosafety>

Genetic Resources Action International: <www.grain.org>

Amazon Link: <www.amazonlink.org>

Notes

1 Food First, 'Voices from the South: The Third World Debunks Corporate Myths on Genetically Engineered Crops' <www.foodfirst.org/progs/global/ge/sactoministerial/voices.php>

2 Martin Leeb, 'Antibiotics: A Shot in the Arm', *Nature*, 431, 7011 (21 October 2004), p. 892 <www.nature.com>; Mike Davis, 'The New Plagues', *Socialist Worker*, 1926 (6 November 2004), <www.socialistworker.co.uk>

3 See N. Suresh and Pradeep S. Mehta, 'No Patents on Life Forms', Consumer Unity and Trust Society of Calcutta, briefing paper, 1995 <www.cuts-international.org>

4 'No Patents on Rice! No Patents on Life!' Statement from peoples' movements and NGOs across Asia, revised August 2001, at <www.grain.org/publications/rice-no-patents-en.cfm>

5 Tewolde Berhan Gebre Egziabher, Director General, Environmental Protection Authority of Ethiopia, 'The African Proposal to the WTO: We Have the Right Not to Patent Life and to Recognize Community Knowledge', July 2003, at <www.grain. org/docs/africa-proposal-wto-tewolde-july-2003–en.pdf>

6 Vandana Shiva, 'Community Rights, People's Sovereignty and Treaties to Reclaim the Genetic and Water Commons', *Synthesis/Regeneration*, 29 (autumn 2002).

7 | No borders! No nations! Stop deportations!

Classical free trade theory confronts Fortress Europe

Capital is two-faced on the issue of labour mobility. Classical free trade theory proposed that in order to maximize the 'comparative advantage' of national production through international trade, capital and labour must be permitted to be as mobile as goods. The point of this is that controlled, cheap labour is not a true 'comparative advantage', a concept reserved for climatic, geographic or other qualities specific to a nation's economy.

With no interest in classical theory, the new regimes of 'free trade' liberate capital while containing labour, manufacturing controlled national advantages in labour costs. This regime facilitates wage suppression in the Global North, as citizen workers are controlled by the threat of replacement by cheaper immigrant and foreign labourers, who in turn are controlled by state terror.

Immigration is one of the most visible results of free trade policies. Structural adjustment in the Global South, particularly dumping which disrupts the agricultural market for peasants, drives the poor to such desperate straits that they are willing to endure the dangers and terrors of migration in order to work clandestinely in the North.

The economic dislocations caused by the disciplines of the new European common market (an FTA), alongside the 'democracy deficit' in which political sovereignty is usurped (albeit unevenly) by a complex and shifting array of new institutions, have led to a resurgence of nationalism. While states and major political parties have cooperated with every step of unification (although at their own pace), popular sentiment has been 'sharply divided at best'.[1] The unsettled populations of Europe have focused their anxieties on immigrants.

7 upper: Brussels, January 2004 (photo by Guido, Belgium Indymedia)
lower: Action against collective deportations at the airport of Brussels, organized by the Vluchtelingen Actie Komitee in the spring of 2004. (photo by VAK, Indymedia Oost-Vlaanderen)

Although European states are indeed alarmed by this resurgence of racism, they also benefit from it as a very confusing distraction from the similarity in circumstances faced by domestic national workers in the Global North and South, who are suffering under the very same 'adjustment' policies. Keeping the people terrified of each other, increasingly separated by government *cordons sanitaires*, also suits corporations nicely, because the labourers of the Global South are thereby kept affordable *wherever* they are and Northern workers – seemingly willing to accept any hardship but multiculturalism – can be continually cheapened and undermined. Simultaneously vilifying and terrorizing immigrants ensures a 'union-proof'[2] working class.

Fortress Europe?[3]

Although it is no secret to governments that 'economic migrants add to economic growth, pay more in taxes than they take in welfare payments (provided they are allowed to be legally employed), and tend to be the brightest and most ambitious members of their communities'[4] governments 'see immigrants as a cause of racism and xenophobia which, in turn, *produce* political instability'.[5] Purportedly to curb the cause of European fascism and xenophobia (by eliminating the immigrants!), the EU is erecting a new border.

The International Organization on Migration (IOM), becoming increasingly powerful in the EU, is accused of institutionalizing racist principles of homogeneous ethnic states and xenophobic concepts of 'home' while controlling people for economic purposes. New EU institutions of Fortress Europe include the Schengen Information System (SIS), founded in 1995 to deal with the problem that, in the absence of internal borders, the EU needed 'a common system to investigate and search for persons and objects', but which in fact works to 'detect and deport non-EU-nationals [and] control the movement of political activists'.[6] Increased technologies of control are making migration more deadly, with 742 deaths of migrants documented between January 2002 and August 2003.[7]

69

While European anti-globalization movements fight many of the effects of regional integration, in taking on the issue of immigration they engage not only the official promoters of free trade policies, but also the psychological support for it in the racism of the North. Thus, while integration has been resisted on many fronts, the most vibrant, creative and confrontational movement responding to integration is the anti-racist campaign to support immigrant rights. Using concepts such as 'no one is illegal', 'no borders', 'the world belongs to everyone',[8] and 'everyone is an expert',[9] this movement has embraced structured North–South inequality at home. These campaigns are perhaps the most advanced manifestation of the visionary humanism and solidarity of the Northern anti-globalization movements. 'Closing the frontiers does nothing to resolve the fundamental issue at stake in immigration – the inequality between North and South.'[10]

The movement in support of immigrant rights has a broad range of tactics, ranging from legal counselling and housing support to antifa youth brigades (who physically protect immigrant communities from both racist attacks and police indifference), invading detention centres in an attempt to free the migrants and close the centres, and interfering with deportations at airports.

Under the cynical slogan 'more control, more exclusion, more deportations', European groups protested the implementation of the Amsterdam Treaty in Tampere/Finland in October 1999. Later in the year, they founded the No Border Network to facilitate the process of collaboration among organizations in many countries, prominent among which were the German 'No One is Illegal' network (founded in 1997 out of other organizations going back to 1994),[11] Autonoom Centrum Amsterdam (founded 1991),[12] the French Sans Papiers Movement (1996),[13] and the Collectif Anti-Expulsions of Paris-Ile de France (founded 1998). European autonomous movements have been tied with the struggles to protect immigrant communities for decades.[14] Throughout the 1990s and up to the present, tens of thousands of people appeared regularly in solidarity with refugees, asylum-seekers and immigrants. This large and diverse social movement takes shape in marches, direct actions and clever campaigns intertwined with anti-globalization and resistance to European integration.

(No)border camps and caravans

The first (no)border camp was held on the Germany–Poland border in 1998. By 2001, there were chains of border camps, including Tijuana, Mexico, and Woomera, Australia.[15] The 'noborder tour 03' visited anti-globalization and EU summits as well as camps. The camps are inseparably spaces of education, action (from demonstrations at agencies to assaults on detention centres, occasionally resulting in the freeing of detainees), 'festivals of resistance' and social experiments in collective and autonomous provisioning.[16]

> Our methods and our goals are education ... but we'll make use of tactical experiments, cunning amusements, and well-aimed irritations ... The fight against borders is a fight against infra-red cameras, plastic handcuffs, and decentralized and diffuse controls along and around the borders. It's also a fight against narrow-mindedness, resentment, and racism ... border protection is possible largely through the ... officially encouraged willingness ... of the population to denounce 'suspicious persons'. To sabotage a border regime means, above all, to disturb this willingness.[17]

Combined education, action and festivity caravans have become a regular feature of anti-globalization organizing. The 'No Border, No Nation, Stop Deportation' tour of 2001 included three political caravans of education and action, visiting five border camps and seven counter-summits, mounting street parties, demonstrations and hi-tech independent media.

> The noborder-caravan will be a mobile campaign for information about the right 'no one is illegal' and the need and experience for direct action in public space ... to combine nomadic travelling, with direct political action, exchanging experiences,

documenting, mediaworking and making of political–artistic festivities. The noborder-caravan should be a political and artistic project and a process of social action-theatre, a new form of cultural discourse.[18]

Interventions and connections

While legal attempts to prevent deportations are important, increasingly migrants and allies alike take direct action. These have included campaigns (in which even uniformed pilots have participated) against the airlines contracted to carry the deported. A clever campaign called 'Deportation Class' aims to bring the attention of regular passengers to the plight of migrants and shame the airline companies.

> We at Deportation Class prefer to speak plain text. We don't conceal what is really happening in the last rows of an airplane, when people are suffocated, tranquillized and fettered, in order to deport them to countries they were once fleeing ... we won't bore you with endless idle talk about global villages, new nomadism and freedom of movement. In the Deportation Class only one value counts: you have to have the wrong passport and then we will treat you with services you have never dreamed about. There are no round-trips and the only way out is manifest resistance.[19]

In France the Collectif Anti-Expulsions of Paris-Ile de France has published a *Guide d'Intervention dans les Aeroports*.[20]

Typical of the anti-globalization movement wherever it appears is the forming of previously missed or avoided connections, bringing to life the Zapatista vision of a world in which 'everyone fits ... where all steps may walk, where all may have laughter, where all may live the dawn'.[21] Such connections are now being made by the Korean anti-globalization movement. The Korean Confederation of Trade Unions includes the Equality Trade Union – Migrants' Branch (founded 2001) in which migrant workers are organized regardless of nationality or industry (despite not being recognized by labour law).[22]

Migrant workers in South Korea, along with irregular workers, street vendors and allies, have organized cultural festivals, rallies and 'Action, action – direct action!',[23] including months-long 'sit-in struggles' in churches. The Migrants' Union is also active in the anti-war and anti-militarism struggles and exhorts: 'Another world is possible, only if you want and fight for it!'[24]

Resources

Everyone is an Expert!: <www.expertbase.net>
Noborder.net: <www.no-racism.net>
No Borders: <www.noborder.org>
Deportation-Class: <www.deportation-class.com>
Equality Trade Union – Migrants' Branch: <migrant.nodong.net>

Notes

1 Manuel Castells, 'European Unification in the Era of the Network State', 12 December 2001 at <OpenDemocracy.net>

2 George Lipsitz, *The Possessive Investment in Whiteness: How White People Profit from Identity Politics* (Philadelphia, PA: Temple University Press, 1998).

3 *Fortress Europe?* Circular Letter at <www.fecl.org>

4 Larry Elliott, 'Fortress Europe Pulls up the Drawbridge', *Guardian*, 3 June 2002.

5 Nigel Harris, *Thinking the Unthinkable: The Immigration Myth Exposed* (London: I.B. Tauris, 2002), my emphasis.

6 'The Schengen Information System: Electronic Instrument of Migration Control and Deportation', 14 December 2001. <www.no-racism.net>

7 Liz Felteke, 'Death at the Border: Who is to Blame?', Institute of Race Relations, 20 August 2003.

8 Autonoom Centrum is an action group in Amsterdam, the Netherlands, focusing on globalization, migration and international conflicts. <www.autonoomcentrum.nl>

9 'Referring to the shift in official immigration-policy and an increasing importance of migrant labour forces for the economic development (in Germany in March 2000 expressed in the government's slogan: "we need it – experts") our association started in 2001 as "everyone is an expert" with the focus to redefine and to reclaim the social dimensions of migration ... we consider communication between multitudinous struggles as a crucial

condition and the autonomy of migration as a driving force in a globalisation from below.' <www.expertbase.net>

10 José Bové, 'A Farmers' International' (November 2001), pp. 137–51 in Tom Mertes (ed.), *A Movement of Movements: Is Another World Really Possible?* (London: Verso, 2004).

11 ag3f, the 'anti-racist group for free flooding' in Hanau (20km east of Frankfurt), was founded at the beginning of the 1990s, the initiative rooted in a project to defend social benefits for all (called 'basta group'). Since 1994 an additional 'refugee's coffeehouse', a kind of counselling office and meeting point, 'was opened in the squatted autonomous centre in our city'. <www. noborder.org/about/members.php>

12 'We have chosen to work there where the conflicting interests of migrants on one side and the government on the other are the most intense. We are one of the only groups in the Netherlands who combine relief work, actions and research.' <www. autonoomcentrum.nl>

13 'The sans-papiers movement began in France in March 1996, when 300 illegal African people (the so-called "sans-papiers") occupied the St Ambroise Church in Paris to obtain regular documents from the French authorities. Ten of them went on hunger strike for fifty-two days. They became famous when the security forces broke down the doors of the Church and forcibly evicted the 300 undocumented Africans.' Marc Chemillier, Sans Papiers webmaster <www.bok.net/pajol>

14 George Katsiaficas, *The Subversion of Politics: European Autonomous Social Movemetns and the Decolonization of Everyday Life* (New Jersey: Humanities Press, 1997).

15 <woomera2002.antimedia.net>

16 Tuebinger Zeltplatzbande at the end of August 2002, 'Camping with the Multitude – a Strasbourg Evaluation' at <www. noborder.org>

17 Border Camp 99 Call for an Action Camp at the German–Polish–Czech Border Triangle 7–15 August 1999, <www.contrast. org/borders/camp>

18 'Austrian Noborder-Platform, Call to Action for European Public Theatre – Caravan with the Campaign Slogan "NO Border – NO Nation – No One is Illegal"', summer 2001, <www.no-racism. net/nobordertour/call_uk.html>

19 <www.deportation-class.com>

20 <www.bok.net/pajol/ouv/cae/index.html>

21 Fourth Declaration of the Lacandon Jungle, 1 January 1996.

22 The situation for migrants worsened considerably in July 2003, when the South Korean parliament created a new regulation concerning migrant workers, limiting them to a three-year stay with annual renewals. The law would mean the immediate deportation of 227,000 workers. 'Employment Permit Bill Passes National Assembly', 2 August 2003, <www.base21.org> Also, there is a report that the police who apprehend migrants for deportation have been issued 'guns with nets' (Hiechul of NFSVK, 31 March 2004, on <www.go.jinbo.net>).

23 Christian Karl, 'South Korea: Migrant Workers' Struggle Reaches Its Apex', 16 November 2003, Labournet, at <www.labournet.net>

24 'Thoughts About Our Common Next Struggles', Equality Trade Union – Migrants' Union at <www.migrant.nodong.net/ver2/index_e.html>

No borders!

8 Hebe de Bonafini, founder of the Madres
de la Plaza de Mayo, marches with *piqueteros*
during the first national mobilization of
piqueteros in Buenos Aires, Argentina, February
2002 (photo by Tim Russo)

8 | Get rid of them all! The importance of Argentina and anti-elitism

December 19, 2001: Frustrated and incensed by the impoverishment of poor and middle classes in a fruitless attempt to pay the external debt racked up by former torturers, Argentines combine to demand the resignation first of the finance minister, then of the president, and the next four replacement presidents ...

Que se vayan todos (Get rid of them all)

The middle classes physically attacked the shuttered banks and joined the angry and festive *cacerolazos*, banging pots and pans, 'symbolizing their inability to purchase the basic necessities of life'.[1]

> In contrast to other uprisings, the Argentines have repudiated not only the economic model but also the ruling class and all the unions, with one or two exceptions ... In the past, demonstrators had always obeyed strike rules, marching in columns behind their union or party banners. This time, they came out simply as citizens. There were no banners, just the national flag ... The few political leaders who tried to join the crowd were rejected.[2]

The redefinition of political landscape had several dimensions. Political consciousness was sharpened through the recognition that the 'solutions' offered by elites would never address the people's needs. Meanwhile, a growing recognition of the limitations of representative politics transformed the institutional practices of the movement itself. Not least, the rapid impoverishment of the middle classes[3] fomented fruitful cross-class experiences and alliances, not only contributing to class-consciousness but also expanding the cultural practices of resistance.

Workers took over viable factories while the unemployed developed enterprises in abandoned ones. Both groups exercised workplace self-management, including principles of direct democracy, horizontality and autonomy.[4] Debates rapidly developed on issues such as whether or not the foreign debt ought to be paid at all – and that it *not* be paid rapidly became the mainstream viewpoint: 'The real excitement came from the level of political discussion. Everywhere people were discussing issues that normally only revolutionary socialists raise – how society can be changed, how to stop the slide into economic chaos and mass impoverishment, and what is to be done about the question of "power".'[5]

But the freezing of bank accounts in December did not start this movement. Argentina's anti-neoliberal paroxysm was built on well-developed political cultures of resistance unique to each social class and sector which participated. These sectors had in common exposure to various socialist debates and parties, a perception of unions as often institutionalized and corrupt, a bad experience with faithful marketization policies and a consequent distrust of all elites,[6] and a number of alternative economic institutions. Since 1990, an extensive community gardening programme had been underway, so that 450,000 gardens were already in service by 2001.[7] These and other experiments with alternative economics and power contributed to the flourishing political cultures of resistance.

Voting is compulsory in Argentina, unless you are 500km from your home on polling day. During the elections of 1999 an anti-capitalist group took several hundred people 501km outside of Buenos Aires, to hold debates about direct democracy and register with an extremely perplexed local police force the fact that they weren't going to vote. In last October's congressional elections, a record 22 per cent cast blank votes or abstained ... This time around many more will abstain. But breaking the law is commonplace now – even the middle classes, or what's left of them, are regularly refusing to pay taxes, or electricity bills.[8]

Alongside these developments, the struggle extended and

popularized two key tactics: road blockades and participatory democratic governance. These tactics were already in use by anti-globalization movements everywhere, but Argentinians creatively established their usefulness in solving a massive financial crisis.

The Argentinian movement, while striking, is not all that novel. Commenting on the recent history of Latin American uprisings, long-time observer James Petras explains that the shift away from state-oriented power and towards new political projects and formations is continent-wide. Socialist, populist and national capitalist parties alike have failed to challenge structural adjustment programmes. All participated in implementing neoliberal policies, and pursued few development projects other than those involving local capitalists.

Class-based movements which have become powerful are composed instead of 'Indian peasants, urban neighborhood committees of unemployed, rural landless workers, precarious workers, public employees, and the poor self-employed'.[9] The social agent formerly conceptualized as the industrial working class is now better characterized as 'mass peasant–indian–urban unemployed ... coalitions engaged in extra-parliamentary activity'.[10]

Such coalitions have already developed a new form of power, founded on their 'independence from electoral party control, their continent-wide scope, their powerful network of solidarity [and] their profound roots in local movements and involvement in concrete struggles'.[11] One result of this movement is that 80 per cent of the population of Latin America 'is opposed to the "new colonialism"'.[12] Petras concludes: 'The historical and empirical evidence demonstrates that the direct action class-based socio-political movements have been the only political forces capable of resisting, reversing or overthrowing neo-liberal regimes and policies.'

Piqueteros and cocaleros

Years before the exciting crisis of December 2001, Argentinian unemployeds rejected by the formal and informal economies alike had discovered how to make economic demands – not by withholding labour, obviously, but by controlling the roads. This movement began in Jujuy in May 1997, spreading quickly through the province and effectively pressuring the government to promise 12,500 new jobs and better unemployment aid. Soon the tactic was used in other cities. In the first half of 1997, there were seventy-seven roadblocks, twenty-three of them in Buenos Aires. In the first half of 2001 there were 1,609 blockades, 1,107 of them in Buenos Aires.[13]

> Once a highway is chosen, the assembly organizes support within the neighborhoods near the road. Hundreds and even thousands of people participate, setting up tents and soup kitchens. The threat of police action swells the crowd.[14]

> They block the roads, demand a specific number of 'plan trabajor', the unemployed subsidies, and more often than not get them from the local government ... They have also used the tactic to back various demands, including getting food from supermarkets. Last Christmas they picketed eight blocks, closing down six supermarkets in one go. They demanded food for the neighbourhood's Christmas dinner. [...]

> Astor's mother had joined the movement before him. He had a job selling loans for new cars, and every time he saw his elderly mother on TV, masked up and blocking the highways, he would cringe with embarrassment. But now no one buys cars and the job disappeared. So one day he went to the piquetero assembly out of curiosity.[15]

The *piqueteros* are well organized by neighbourhood. Participation in meetings and actions are the basis of distributing resources, along with an assessment of need.[16] They also are engaged in education and provisioning. Through self-organization the *piqueteros* have established autonomous zones, including parallel economies. In one town, General Mosconi, more than 300 projects, including bakeries, organic gardens, water-purifying plants and clinics, have been developed.

As significant as their tactic of power *vis-à-vis* the state is the way in which they use the power. Wary of trade union leadership and representative democracy, they practise autonomy and make all decisions collectively with all members. 'The piqueteros have learned from experience that sending representatives to negotiate in a government office downtown leads to jobs for those individuals, their relatives and their friends, but not necessarily anyone else. [As a result of this recognition] the unemployed demand that the talks occur at the blockade so all the piqueteros can participate.'[17] This ensures, among other things, that the power will not be 'reined in behind a moderate agenda'[18] – or, worse yet, disappear with unaccountable and changeable elites as in the January 2000 Ecuadorian revolution and again in the subsequent election of Lucio Gutiérrez in 2002.[19]

Participatory democracy has also had a huge impact on women:

> It's mostly women who do the speaking at the assemblea. Earlier, Anna had told to me how women are the ones who are hit hardest by unemployment ... women, many of them elderly, many of whom had never had the possibility to make decisions or express important things about their lives, were able to put up their hand and talk freely and people would listen to them. They would propose good ideas and then they would then go into the streets for their children's sake.[20]

Likewise, in the Peruvian anti-privatization struggles of 2002, women were at the forefront of barricade-building.[21]

Meanwhile, in Bolivia, the *cocaleros* (coca growers) have organized a political party which is now the second strongest in that country.[22] (The leader, Evo Morales, almost won the presidency in 2002.) Under pressure from the USA (using financial aid as blackmail), the government still attempts to criminalize the production of coca, although most of it is produced for domestic Bolivian consumption and *campesinos* have no alternative crop. While the party has required Congress to do business in four indigenous languages, their power is on the

Movement toward Socialism — Political Instrument for the Sovereignty of the People (Bolivian political party of the *Cocaleros*) 'Call for National Mobilization', December 2002

1. Recuperation of the property of hydrocarbons to put them at the service of the people and commit the government to not export natural gas to Chile (and the United States as a consequence) ...

2. Recuperation of the privatized multinational industries due to proven corruption and the return of privatized mines in Huanuni and Vinto ...

3. A solution to the land and territory problem with the goal that every Bolivian, especially those without land, and the original peoples, will have land to work ...

4. A pause in the forced eradication of coca leaf in the Chapare, rejecting the eradication of even a single coca leaf in the Yungas region and the demilitarization of the coca growing regions ...

5. Rejection of Bolivia's joining the FTAA, an instrument of colonization of our peoples. To struggle for the strengthening of the regional integration of Latin America ...

6. Rejection of the presence of US troops in Bolivian territory.

streets and in solidarity with movements of pensioners and students against privatization. In October 2003, opposing the sale of natural gas, a popular uprising forced the resignation of the president.

Asembleas and Bolivarian Circles

In Argentina, the redefinition of political landscape, combined with the tremendous need for local provisioning, has produced an impressive experiment with local self-governance. People began holding meetings in their neighbourhood in order to collaborate in survival. The collaborations rapidly extended into productive and celebratory aspects of life, such as seizing a printing plant to print their own texts. 'The members of the Asembleas movement in Argentina repeat daily that their lives have been transformed from passivity and consumption into active engagement of everyday life by the directly democratic and anti-hierarchical asembleas.'[23]

When the winter came, the *asembleas* started taking over buildings (a good use for the old banks), creating meeting space and local centres to share meals, information and skills.[24] The formerly middle-class *asembleas* have realized that they are not very different from the formerly working-class *piqueteros* movement, and have increasingly worked alongside them and shared resources.[25]

As a result of the successful and extensive development of spaces of self-government and self-provisioning, there is little interest in or need for the state. The only interest in the 2003 elections was the opportunity taken by Luis Zamora's movement.

> When asked what he will do if he is elected, Zamora says he wouldn't last a day and that he doesn't want to be president anyway. 'Go self-determine yourself,' he says. 'Take care of yourself, take it in your own hands, if you don't take it in your own hands, nothing is going to change.' He describes what is happening in Argentina as 'a revolution in the heads of millions' ... a situation where the 'population is doing politics' rather than the politicians.[26]

This attitude of independence from political parties and the state is found throughout the anti-globalization movement. Farmers' organizer José Bové explains that 'it's a condition of membership of the Confédération Paysanne that you cannot stand in an election ... The aim of a social movement or a union like ours is to enable people to act for themselves.'[27]

In Venezuela, in order to defend the 1999 constitution, President Chávez called for 'people to get organized and to fight for their rights' through the organization of Bolivarian Circles which are 'the most basic form of participation in the democratic process'. Specifically this means 'people being able to directly design, supervise and carry out their development projects without intermediaries, without people representing them'. The Circles are autonomous and avoid leaders. They responded to the attempted coup against Chávez by taking 'control of different parts of the country' and reversed it.[28]

Similarly, after throwing out the president in October 2003, the Bolivian movements have increasingly focused their efforts on 'positive proposals, instead of always just fighting against bad government policies'. To hand for this process is the tool made popular in 1999 of 'semi-direct democracy' in which elected officials are elected first by their communities, independent of the official political process. They are held accountable for implementing 'specific proposals' through 'massive popular demonstrations and marches'.[29]

In Ecuador when indigenous peoples and others took over the government in January 2000, a system of *parlamentos populares* was already in place. These were promptly declared the national government in place of all three branches of the previous one. Although promptly reversed by elites trusted by the movements (confirming the need to 'get rid of them all!'), this move modelled a mechanism for preparing direct democratic control.

James Petras is wary of movements like Argentina's which 'are not able to construct a political alternative – with the result that the heroic struggles and mass protests have not led to a serious challenge for state power'. Nevertheless, he argues that 'the uneven development of the mass popular struggle' in Latin America has already demonstrated 'that US imperialism can be defeated'.[30]

Resources

PGA Argentina page: < www.nadir.org/nadir/initiativ/agp/free/imf/argentina>

Argentina IMC: <www.argentina.indymedia.org>

Struggle in Bolivia PGA pages: <www.nadir.org/nadir/initiativ/agp/ free/imf/bolivia/txt/2003/index.htm>

In Defense of Marxism, reporting on Latin America: <www.marxist. com/latinamerica.asp>

Notes

1 Roger Burbach, 'Throw Them All Out: Argentina's Grassroots Rebellion', *Redress Information & Analysis*, 2 July 2002. <www.redress.btinternet.co.uk>

2 Carlos Gabetta, 'Argentina: IMF Show State Revolts', *Le Monde Diplomatique*, January 2002.

3 By mid-2002, over half the population was living below the poverty line.

4 Marcel Idels, 'Lula, Chávez and One Very Thorny "Bush": Revolution and the Demise of US Hegemony in Latin America' at <www.print.indymedia.org> 4 March 2003.

5 Chris Harman, 'Argentina: Swimming with the Tide of Revolt', *Socialist Review*, 263 (May 2002).

6 An October 2002 poll found 95 per cent disapproval of all political parties and 90 per cent dissatisfaction with the Congress, the markets, the banks and the judicial system (Peter Greste, BBC, 'Democracy Has Failed Say Argentines', 3 October 2002 at <www.news.bbc.co.uk/1/hi/world/americas/2296621.stm>).

7 The Federal PRO-HUERTA programme was founded in 1990. (See Jac Smit, 'Urban Agriculture, Progress and Prospect: 1975–2005', Urban Agriculture Network [TUAN] Report 18, *Cities Feeding People Series* [March 1996] IDRC, Canada.)

8 John Jordan, 'Que Se Vayan Todos: Argentina's Popular Rebellion' at <www.nadir.org/nadir/initiativ/agp/free/imf/ argentina/txt/2002/0918que_se_vayan.htm> February and August 2002.

9 James Petras, 'Class-based Direct Action Versus Populist Electoral Politics', *Rebelión*, March 2004. For an explanation of Lula Da Silva's resistance to WTO and ALCA as support for Brazil's agrarian elite, not small farmers, see 'Brazil and the FTAA', *Rebelión*, September 2003.

10 Ibid.

11 Ibid.

12 James Petras, 'Present Situation in Latin America', *Rebelión*, 6 June 2003.

13 Statistics from a study by the New Majority Studies Center, reported in Gerardo Young and Lucas Guagnini, 'Argentina's New Social Protagonists', published first in *Clarin* with added content in *World Press Review* (December 2002).

14 James Petras, 'Road Warriors Blocking Highways Throughout Argentina, Unemployed Workers Lead a Promising Movement for Basic Change', <www.Americas.org> February 2002.

15 Jordan, 'Que Se Vayan Todos'.

16 Young and Guagnini, 'Argentina's New Social Protagonists'.

17 Petras, 'Road Warriors Blocking Highways'.

18 Ibid.

19 Jorge Martín, 'Lucio with the IMF, the Masses Against Lucio', *In Defense of Marxism*, 12 December 2003 at <www.marxist.com>

20 Jordan, 'Que Se Vayan Todos'.

21 Jordi Martorell, 'Peru – Mass Uprising Defeats Privatisation Plans', *In Defense of Marxism*, 24 June 2002. at <www.marxist.com>

22 The first national meeting of the MAS including both the members of Congress and the bases, after the failed negotiations with the government, took place on 26–28 December, Chimoré. Luis Gómez, 'Fighting for Life: Boliva's Coca Growers Lead a New Mobilization', *Narco News Bulletin*, 27, 15 January 2003. <www.narconews.com>

23 t, WSF-PDX IMCista, 'Part 4: The Movement of Movements & Update on the Casa de Indy', <www.portland.indymedia.org> 25 January 2003.

24 Jordan, 'Que Se Vayan Todos'.

25 Ibid.

26 Ibid.

27 José Bové, 'A Farmers' International' (November 2001), pp. 137–51 in Tom Mertes (ed.), *A Movement of Movements: Is Another World Really Possible?* (London: Verso, 2004).

28 Rodrigo Chaves and Tom Burke, 'The Bolivarian Circles', *ZNet*, 30 July 2003 at <www.zmag.org>

29 Susan Harvie, 'Wind of Democratic Change in Bolivia', *Alternatives*, 8, 6 (6 March 2004) at <www.alternatives.ca>

30 Petras, 'Present Situation in Latin America'.

9 | *Solidarité* and *specifismo*: we are going to work together

International solidarity has been a strategic goal for social justice movements for a very long time. Not only have labour and socialist organizations relied upon international solidarity, but so have campaigns to end slavery, women's rights movements, struggles against fascism, anti-colonial struggles and the anti-apartheid movements. During the 1970s and 1980s, grassroots North–South alliances proliferated, taking on a range of tasks from confronting militarization to sharing sustainable technologies. Indigenous people, meeting and organizing ever more widely, declared their rights in the form of a United Nations declaration.

Through these movements, relationships and analyses have been developed across vast geographic, socioeconomic and cultural distances. In this experience, problems of paternalism and cooptation have been confronted with increasing sophistication. The anti-globalization movement developed along the routes of these established connections, rapidly cross-fertilizing. Vía Campesina describes itself as not only 'a real farmers' International' but also as 'a living example of a new relationship between North and South'.[1]

These collaborations illuminate the connections between local and global problems. Militarism, poverty, unemployment, discrimination, hunger, exploitation, endangerment of indigenous peoples, environmental degradation, dams, mines and food quality are no longer seen as separate problems but as manifestations of the same processes. The struggles against each of these issues are increasingly interwoven.

So the WTO's 'constitution for a new global economy' was greeted by a 'unity of many determinations'.[2] Collaborators called their shared enemy many names: 'globalization', 'corporate power', 'neoliberalism', 'corporate globalization',

9 Manifestations against the WTO, Cancún, Mexico, September 2003 (image from activist media project 2004 *This is What Free Trade Looks Like*)

'capitalist globalization' and, increasingly, 'imperialism'. 'What we are seeing today is a movement that, for the first time, is adopting the same perspectives, hitting at the same targets, and developing all over the world, linking local struggles to global objectives.'[3] The earlier movements built solidarity through the steady processes of international work, travel brigades, pressure campaigns, fundraising, speaking tours and the like. A few new methods of solidarity have been developed in and through the anti-globalization movement.

Zapatismo

The Ejército Zapatista Liberación Nacional (EZLN) of Chiapas, Mexico, is often credited for catalysing resistance to the free trade era of globalization. Their resistance inspired movements around the world. The Zapatistas distinguished themselves by an unwillingness to use their weapons offensively while holding their own against large portions of the Mexican military and simultaneously building autonomous political and economic institutions. They shared their ideas in compelling and intriguing political theory and welcomed outsiders to work and study in the communities.

Several aspects of this political theory strongly influenced the understanding of solidarity in the anti-globalization movement. One of the most striking Zapatista concepts is the assessment that indigenous knowledge is relevant to postmodern society and its problems. This assertion was, among other things, a pre-emptive strike against paternalism.

As sympathizers from all over the world sought to assist the Zapatistas in their struggle against globalization, they were exhorted to locate points of impact in their own cities and cultures and then elaborate Zapatismo there. This illustrates David Graeber's point that 'globalization from below' differs from previous internationalisms in that, rather than 'exporting Western organizational models ... the flow has if anything been the other ways around'.[4] Brian Dominick articulates a framework for Northern Zapatismo:

In the 1980s and a little before, solidarity almost always meant ... that we send stuff to these other countries that were in need. We were trying to offset the horrible things that our military and our economic system were doing by saying we're going to send people for 'protective accompaniment', and ... medical supplies and other things like that ... But the Zapatistas decided to say 'That's great, that's really cool, we want all that stuff ... But when you come, learn.' And that's one thing: solidarity cannot be unilateral ... Solidarity for the Zapatistas meant, first and foremost, that we're kicking ass here at home. They said: 'We can hold these folks for a little while longer, but if you can remove the boot from our neck by stopping your society from funding our government who is doing it directly to us, then, boy, wouldn't that be a big relief? ... Then, please go home and organize ... not just against imperialism and the massive military expenditures going to support the war in México, but against the shit that you need to recognize as your own problems. Stop letting us distract you from the fact that your cities have third worlds in them, that racism and sexism, things that we are really beginning to get a grip on here, are rampant in your home. Go home and take care of that.'[5]

The Zapatistas also recognized what social movements scholars call the importance of 'identity' to social movements, welcoming everyone to call themselves a Zapatista.[6] The eloquent Subcomandante Marcos wove myths of collective political identity to support new cultures of resistance, imagining himself as 'every untolerated oppressed, exploited minority' (gay in San Francisco, Palestinian in Israel, a housewife in any neighbourhood in any city in any part of Mexico on a Saturday night).[7] Movements all over the world responded, '*Todos somos Marcos*' (We are all Marcos).

The electronic fabric of struggle

While many commentators have either blithely credited the internet for making the struggle possible or dismissed it as the master's tool, a few have sought to define its role precisely.

One of these is Harry Cleaver, who argues that the power of the internet 'has lain in connection and circulation, in the way widely dispersed nodes of antagonism set themselves in motion in response' to international events. Virtual organizing was already in use in the North American struggle against NAFTA. The same networks then carried news of the Zapatista uprising and their messages. Clearly, the internet facilitates inexpensive circulation of information – among those who have computer technology. But its independent contribution to arousing mobilization is not clear. According to Cleaver, its limits 'lie both in the limits of the reach of The Net ... and in the kinds of connections established'.[8]

Cleaver remarks on elite panics over the internet's contribution to 'ungovernability' and 'excessive democracy'. Its continued usefulness as political space for movements depends upon it being actively defended against commodification and privatization. It is protected by many of its workers who are 'dedicated to the free flow of ideas and exchange of imagination'. They have engendered an ongoing 'struggle over the content, and thus the nature' of that space, such that 'every piece of hardware and software is subject to the subversion of the purposes for which it was designed'.

Another powerful electronic tactic has been the activist video network. Armed with digital video cameras and laptop editing systems, activists from the Global North have been able to produce, and distribute video clips and films to share news of global struggles vividly and rapidly. Operating outside the network of independent art films (viewed only at elite film festivals), activist videos are distributed as widely as possible and at the lowest possible cost.

Working through the Independent Media Network, Northern video activists have assisted in the development of activist video in the Global South, sharing equipment and training so that Southern activists can tell their own stories. And the electronic fabric of struggle does not simply connect North and South; the majority of videos made by the Chiapas Media Project/Promedios de Comunicación Comunitaria are in

91

indigenous languages and do not leave the region; they are used to share strategies among the communities in resistance.

Global carnivals

Starting in 1998, a series of 'global days of action' produced a new method of connection between dispersed social movements. The events took many different forms, from gardening in roadways and street parties to traditional demonstrations and campaign kick-offs. But as important as the local message was the power of connection – both experientially and strategically – in a simultaneous global action against the same, named, enemy.

The framework of simultaneous action fostered events which illustrated the local effects of globalization while also drawing attention to struggles far away. The abstractions of globalization were made concrete and the powerful experience of solidarity was extended to people outside the formal organizations which had hosted solidarity experiences in the past.

The first 'global carnival', 16 May 1998 (m16), involved simultaneous actions in thirty countries on the occasion of the Second WTO Ministerial in Geneva.[9] The second 'global carnival' took place on 18 June 1999 (j18) on the occasion of the G8 meeting in Cologne. On j18 the most dramatic of the global actions (in forty-three countries) was in the City of London, 'the heart of the global economy'.[10]

The third global action day was 30 November 1999 (n30), when the WTO tried to meet for its third Ministerial in Seattle. By 15 February 2003 this tactic had developed to the point that 16 million persons disrupted 133 cities to say, 'The World Says No to War'. Acts which would otherwise feel and appear marginal gained tremendous significance as part of this framework. G8 meetings and WTO Ministerials continue to be some of the major occasions for global days of action and <www.protest.net> tries to keep track of both local and global protests.

Making the connections

The anti-globalization movement is often conceptually reduced to the global days of action, which are then scorned as symbolic acts irrelevant to local organizations, or as the militant self-expression of disaffected youth, or escapist play ('summit hopping', 'protest tourism'). Activists who participate in these actions are ridiculed for supposedly preferring glamour and drama to ordinary, local struggles.

Activists argue that local and global action cannot be separated. Starhawk explains: 'Many of us have come to the larger, global actions because we understand that the trade agreements and institutions we contest are designed to undo all of our local work and override the decisions and aspirations of local communities.'[11] Massimo De Angelis explains that the struggle against globalization requires both local struggles, where 'our desires and aspirations take shape' and the increasingly global context of struggle, which is fundamentally the 'discovery of the other'.[12]

Indeed, if there is one aspect of struggle which distinguishes anti-globalization it is the act of imagination needed to 'make the connections' between the suffering of people far away and problems and events in one's own community. There are several methods for exercising this imagination.

• Identifying the policies of neoliberalism in their various forms in different contexts by linking community crises to the larger processes of globalization. 'It is still very difficult to explain to an unemployed youngster of 18 all the connexions between his immediate plight and the role of the IMF or WTO.'[13] These connections include: sweatshops in the Global South and plant closures in the Global North; desperate migrants and Structural Adjustment Programmes; unsafe food and free trade 'harmonization'; poverty and tariffs; 'international competitiveness' and attacks on unions and wages; cost of living and privatization: corporate mergers and the loss of cultural space. For example 'ATTAC defines enlargement as a structural-adjustment plan, along

Solidarité and specifismo

IMF lines, for Eastern Europe ... Things could be done in the name of "Europe" that would never have got through otherwise. In this sense, "Europe" was the Trojan horse of neoliberalism in France.'[14]

- Chasing particular corporations from particular destructive projects in the Global South to their headquarters in the North, drawing attention to their dangerous activities and products, their irresponsibility towards worker and ecology, their seductive and misleading advertising and power plays.

- Creating new institutions and practices which transform, from the ground up, the relations of production (e.g. Fair Trade, reconnecting electricity, producer cooperatives). As people become involved in such projects – initially as an alternative solution to an immediate problem or concern – they discover the multiple and global dimensions of their problem and the viability of alternatives.

We have to build where we are ... what are the problems facing people on the ground that unite us most? In Soweto, it's electricity. In another area, it is water ... But you have to build with a vision. From Day One we argued that electricity cuts are the result of privatization. Privatization ... reflects the demands of global capital ... We cannot finally win this immediate struggle unless we win that greater one. But still, connecting with what touches people on a daily basis, in a direct fashion, is the way to move history forward.[15]

- Imagining global subjectivity through the similarities of experience, and recognizing the shared opportunities and techniques of struggle.

The villagers stand up to their waist in the water, the rising waters threatening to drown them, as it has drowned their very way of life. Their hands are raised in prayer position as they enact their morning ritual of thanks to the river, of apology to the river, of thanks to the Buddha. Each night, another ceremony is dedicated to their brothers and sisters in the struggle at the Narmada Dam in India.[16]

Privileged activists in a global movement

The damage caused by globalization and the rush of passionate solidarity have recuperated universalism. This universalism can be analytically useful and can strengthen solidarity. It can also obscure oppressive practices within social movements. For those who have been privileged in some sense, the ongoing process of decolonization requires a constant investigation of internalized oppression, which often manifests as paternalism. This paternalism can be revolutionary, it can create martyrs, it can be self-effacing and sacrificial, but it is still paternalism.

Internalized oppression operates at many levels. A few examples: it is often difficult for educated activists to support projects which do not satisfy their political analysis. (They sometimes label these projects 'reformist'.) Such arrogant judgement of urgent grassroots projects could be seen as a pathology of privilege. One solution offered to this problem is to give privilege to the perspectives of people who are most oppressed in the framing and organizing process.

Decolonizing oneself means getting used to the concept that humanizing transformations are a function of grassroots power, not correct ideology, good ideas, clever campaigns or efficient logistics. For privileged people, decolonization means getting used to not being the expert. It means not using oppressed people to prove arguments, legitimize projects or facilitate psychic healing. It requires a profound acceptance that the privileged are not the intellectual centre of this revolt. There is still plenty of work that we can get involved with. For example, privileged people can raise funds to pay for Global South activists to attend the World Social Forum instead of attending themselves, decentring Northern omniscience in favour of grassroots Global South connections.

Arguing that the core aspiration of the anti-globalization movement is rejection of the forced choice between the market and the state, instead embracing 'respect, dignity, grassroots democracy and exercise of real power', De Angelis urges activists to move from debates over the 'ethical correctness' of particular acts to an evaluation of 'whether that action

Solidarité and specifismo

was a responsible action in that context'. What, then, is 'responsibility'?

> Responsibility is above all a relationship to the other, one that presupposes the belonging in a community ... Irresponsibility is not a light criticism, precisely because it presupposes their inclusion in our struggle. You can be (ir)responsible only towards your community, not towards some outside force or some grand ethical concept ... And if you are irresponsible towards the 'other' in your community, then think twice, because the world we are fighting against is based precisely on this persistent indifference to the other.[17]

For example, the framework of 'cultural diversity' does not always make a comfortable space for cultures of resistance with different manifestations of dignity. For privileged North American activists, an 'empowering space' is one which allows for individual self-expression assuming horizontality and equity, while for many activists of colour or working-class activists, an empowering space is one which is safe from daily experiences of racism and violence. Moreover, the very concept of *counter*culture blinds participants to oppressive structures internalized within it.

As we become a global community of activists, we develop solidarity through a 'creative process of discovery, not a presumption'.[18] Tolerance in the form of assumed horizontality is not discovery, it is indifference. Fairness arbitrated by abstract ethics is likewise indifferent. Solidarity must be more than *allowing* one another to exist in the indifference of 'diversity of tactics'; supportive direct action requires *knowing* one another.

Specifismo

The Latin American practice of *specifismo* is an excellent example of the solidarity politics of anti-globalization. This concept enables highly ideological groups, such as platformist anarchists, to find a way of contributing to large-scale resistance by working 'inside the social movements', neither demanding ideological concordance from those movements nor abandoning their own politics: 'political groups ... should enhance the social and popular movements, but without trying to make it "anarchist" ... it is possible to unite militants and build a unified base, which is not possible in an ideological level'.[19]

Specifismo brings to life what Northern scholars had vaguely termed a 'politics of difference' in which those differences are maintained while collective work is also engaged. The Zapatistas affirmed the possible coexistence of unity and diversity and their practice inspired renewed efforts.

In addition to a fresh flexibility among many ideological groups, *specifismo* is practised by groups who don't use that term but who prioritize grounded direct action and movement-building over correct theory in order to create and protect solidarity and collective action.

Resources

Zapatismo: Midnight Notes Collective, *Auroras of the Zapatistas: Local & Global Struggles of the Fourth World War* (Autonomedia, 2001).

All the latest Zapatismo including Radio Insurgente at <www.ezln.org>

Communiqués at <www.flag.blackened.net/revolt/México/ezlnco.html>

Subcomandante Marcos, *Shadows of Tender Fury: The Letters and Communiqués of Subcomandante Marcos and the Zapatista Army of National Liberation*, trans. Leslie Lopez, Frank Bardacke and John Ross (New York: Monthly Review Press, 1995).

John Ross, *The War Against Oblivion: Zapatista Chronicles* 1994–2000 (Monroe, ME: Common Courage Press, 2000).

Global carnivals: <www.nadir.org/nadir/initiativ/agp/mayday1.htm>

Protest Net: <www.protest.net>

Electronic fabric: Mark C. Taylor, *The Moment of Complexity: Emerging Network Culture* (Chicago, IL: University of Chicago Press, 2002).

Video activism: Organic Chaos Network for video activism (Netherlands) <www.antenna.nl/organicchaos/shop.html>

Video activist network (USA): <www.videoactivism.org>

Solidarité and specifismo

Chiapas Media Project/Promedios de Comunicación Comunitaria: <promedios.org>

Networks: Sanjeev Khagram et al. (eds), *Restructuring World Politics: Transnational Social Movements, Networks, and Norms*, vol. 14 of *Social Movements, Protest, and Contention* (Minneapolis: University of Minnesota Press, 2002).

Jackie Smith and Hank Johnston (eds), *Globalization and Resistance: Transnational Dimensions of Social Movements* (Lanham, MD: Rowman and Littlefield, 2002).

Privilege: Amory Starr, 'Grumpywarriorcool: What Makes Our Movements White?', in Anthony J. Nocella and Steven Best (eds), *Igniting a Revolution: Voices in Defense of Mother Earth* (Oakland, CA: AK Press, forthcoming).

Notes

1 José Bové, 'A Farmers' International' (November 2001), pp. 137–51 in Tom Mertes (ed.), *A Movement of Movements: Is Another World Really Possible?* (London: Verso, 2004).

2 Karl Marx, *Grundrisse* (1939–41).

3 Bernard Cassen, 'Inventing ATTAC' (January 2003), pp. 152–74 in Mertes (ed.), *A Movement of Movements*.

4 David Graeber, 'The New Anarchists', pp. 202–15 in ibid.

5. Brian Dominick, 'Anti-Capitalist Globalization Organizing', *Arise! Journal* (June 2001).

6. This invitation had to be rescinded in August 2003 due to the misuse of the name 'zapatista' by dishonest people for purposes of banditry and swindling. Now 'only those persons, communities, cooperatives and producers and marketing associations which are registered' with a regional zapatista junta 'shall be recognized as zapatistas' (Subcomandante Insurgente Marcos, 'Chiapas: The Thirteenth Stele. Part Six: A Good Government', July 2003).

7. Consistent with the myth of Marcos, this quote has been modified, elaborated, and reposted but is nowhere cited, and I was unable to find the original in any of the archives.

8 Harry Cleaver, 'The Zapatistas and the Electronic Fabric of Struggle', in John Holloway and Eloína Peláez (eds), *Zapatista! Reinventing Revolution in Mexico* (London: Pluto, 1998). Online at <www.eco.utexas.edu/faculty/Cleaver/zaps.html>

9 <www.nadir.org/nadir/initiativ/agp/en/PGAInfos/bulletin2/bulletin2b.htm>

10 18 June 1999, <www.bak.spc.org/j18>

11 Starhawk, 'After Genoa: Why We Need to Stay in the Streets', August 2001 at <www.starhawk.org/activism/activism-writings/aftergenoa.html>

12 Massimo De Angelis, 'From Movement to Society', pp. 109–24 in *On Fire: The Battle of Genoa and the Anti-capitalist Movement* (London: One-off Press, 2001), pp. 118–19, 124.

13 Cassen, 'Inventing ATTAC'.

14 Ibid.

15 Trevor Ngwane, 'Sparks in the Township' (July 2003), pp. 111–34 in Mertes (ed.), *A Movement of Movements*.

16 Velcrow Ripper, 'Power Generation: The Protest Villages of Thailand', pp. 140–47, in Notes from Nowhere (ed.), *We are Everywhere* (London: Verso, 2003).

17 Massimo De Angelis, 'From Movement to Society', pp. 118–19, 124.

18 Ibid.

19 'The Global Influence of Platformism Today: Brazil: NEFAC Interviews the Federacao Anarquista Gaucha (FAG)', *Northeastern Anarchist*, no. 6, 26 February 2003.

10 Israel Defence Forces patrol occupied
Dheheisheh refugee camp on the outskirts
of Bethlehem in the West Bank, Palestine.
Resistance is Not Terrorism is painted on
the walls behind the IDF and the photo is
taken through a bullet hole of a neighbouring
building. July 2002 (photo by Tim Russo)

10 | Anti-imperialism: anti-globalization since 9/11

For the first few months after 9/11, the future of the anti-globalization movement was unclear. The sweeping abrogations of civil rights pushed by the USA and implemented all over the world[1] seemed to be a direct attack on the movement. Analysing and responding to the 'war on terrorism' (WOT) was a new pile of work, but 'the war on terrorism just strengthened our determination not to be intimidated'.[2]

While some anti-globalization activists hoped the WOT would collapse under the weight of its own historical amnesia or be laughed off the international policy agenda, others jumped into the growing anti-war movements. By the time the WOT had entrenched itself, the anti-globalization movement had transformed itself into a movement which rejected not only corporate globalization but also militarism and US unilateralism.

For Global South activists and others who already equated globalization with colonialism and US militarism, an anti-imperialist analysis was obvious and often already part of their anti-globalization framework. For some activists in the Global North, it was necessary to reintegrate a theory of the state into the analysis of globalization. 'No Blood for Oil' – a radical analysis mainstreamed by the anti-war movements – clarified the motivations of the war. Yet more important was the moment at which it became clear that the 'reconstruction' of Iraq was a rapid and rapacious implementation of structural adjustment – with instant privatization and devastating import liberalization.[3]

In some ways, what 9/11 accomplished was to accelerate the unification of critical social movements focused on material issues (economy, environment, agriculture) with those focused on political issues (sovereignty, repression, militarism). Of

**Direct Action to Stop the War, San Francisco, USA
'Our Goals', May 2003**

1) End the war for empire and uproot the system be-hind it. War for empire includes three interlocking parts: Military war and occupation, including: US military presence throughout the world and support for war and occupation through other regimes. Economic war to impose corporate globalization on the world, including: the IMF, World Bank, WTO, NAFTA, FTAA, CAFTA, and Middle East Free Trade Agreement. War at home, including: racial injustice, sexism and patriarchy; cuts in and privatization of basic services; environmental injustice and ecological destruction; and attacks on civil liberties, immigrants, low-income communities, communities of color, unions, waged and unwaged workers.

2) Impose real economic, social and political costs on governments and corporations and stop business as usual until the war for empire ends.

3) Assert our power to transform our communities and the world from profits, oil and war to resistance and life! We work to create open, welcoming, inspiring spaces where the voices of the anti-war majority can be heard through real, direct democracy.

Why We Target Corporations: We hold corporations including Bechtel, Citigroup, the Carlyle Group and ChevronTexaco accountable not only for their profits from this war, but the fact that they made this war possible through their investments, operations, weapons, lobbying, political contributions and drive for unending profits regardless of the toll on human life, the environment or society.

course, the connections were impossible to ignore for communities already beset with low- or high-intensity responses to their resistance to oil projects, dams, forestry, mining or other projects of corporate globalization.

In the heart of the empire, the organization ANSWER (Act Now to Stop War and End Racism) is largely to be credited with convincing opponents of war to focus on imperialism. ANSWER has historicized the struggle and linked the invasion and occupation of Iraq with imperialist threats to Venezuela, Colombia, the Balkans, Cuba, the Philippines and Palestine.

9/11 and the resulting wars, full of transparent lies and 'bullying', brought the economic and militaristic analyses to a sudden and urgent union. The connections, while sickening, just made more and more sense. Iraq has water to privatize too? Is Bechtel (which tried to privatize Bolivia's water) involved? Yes! ... and Vivendi water is in Bosnia ... The puzzle becomes a pattern.

It was not new for some activists to be explaining the connections between corporate exploitation and militarism, but it certainly was new for such anti-imperialism to be widespread in popular non-socialist movements.

Making these connections revealed a skeleton in the closet – the absence of the Middle East from discussions of globalization. Now, instead of a silence about the region there are many attempts to understand the specific histories of colonialism and client regimes, and the relationships between fundamentalism and imperialism. Meanwhile, the Anti-Globalization Egyptian Group has joined the global movement, challenging Middle East meetings of the World Economic Forum, World Bank interventions and corporate profiteering in Iraq.[4]

By September 2003, the main day of protest against the WTO Ministerial in Cancún was named 'Worldwide Day of Action Against Corporate Globalization and Militarism'. In 2004, anti-globalization activists and other anti-war activists launched the campaign 'Democracy vs. Empire' in San Francisco. The 'proactive, ongoing local campaign of education, movement building and resistance' is focused on the point that 'America cannot be both an empire and a democracy'.[5] Demands of the late 2004 Korean General Strike against neoliberal policies included 'a stop to the extension of deploying South Korean troops to Iraq'.[6]

Of course, throughout the anti-war struggle, the IMF and World Bank continued meeting and adjusting. 'Behind the military conflict there is often a far more cunning and destructive form of economic colonization going on, through the programmes imposed by the IMF and World Bank.'[7] And every action against them is now also against war and the occupation of Iraq and Palestine.

Resources

John Pilger, *The New Rulers of the World* (London: Verso, 2002).

Ellen Meiksins Wood, *Empire of Capital* (London: Verso, 2003).

Noam Chomsky, *Year 501: The Conquest Continues* (Boston, MA: South End Press, 1993).

William Blum, *Killing Hope: U.S. Military and CIA Interventions Since World War II* (Monroe, ME: Common Courage Press, 2003).

P. W. Singer, *Corporate Warriors: The Rise of the Privatized Military Industry* (Ithaca, NY: Cornell University Press, 2003).

Anti-Globalization Egyptian Group: <www.ageg.net>

Notes

1 Leo Panitch, 'Whose Violence? Imperial State Security and the Global Injustice Movement', *Socialist Project*, Socialism Pamphlet Series no. 2, November 2004, at <www.socialistproject.ca>

2 Bernard Cassen, 'Inventing ATTAC' (January 2003), pp. 152–74 in Tom Mertes (ed.), *A Movement of Movements: Is Another World Really Possible?* (London: Verso, 2004).

3 Naomi Klein, 'Privatization in Disguise', *The Nation*, 10 April 2003. <www.thenation.com> David Bacon, 'Umm Qasr – From National Pride to War Booty', *CorpWatch*, 15 December 2003 at <www.corpwatch.org>

4 Issandr El Amrani, 'The Anti-Globalization Movement Comes to Egypt and Finds Eager Friends', *Cairo Times*, 6, 32 (17–23 October 2002).

5 Direct Action to Stop the War, San Francisco. <www.acta-gainstwar.org>

6 Korean Confederation of Trade Unions, 'The KCTU Congress Calls for General Strike', 5 November 2004 at <www.kctu.org>

7 José Bové, 'A Farmers' International' (November 2001), pp. 137–51 in Tom Mertes (ed.), *A Movement of Movements*.

Anti-imperialism

THREE | **Controversies**

This is what democracy looks like

In Seattle, self-conscious of our dishevelment in the rain and aware of our confusing assemblage of signage, we chanted '*This* is what *democracy* looks like!' We were an excellent contrast with the orderly but exclusionary WTO. In the latter days of the protest, we alternated the chant with '*That* is what a *police state* looks like!'

'This is what democracy looks like' means we're not done yet. We're still in the process. In fact we're still disagreeing, sometimes vehemently. It means we don't even have the *process* completely worked out yet! But it also asserts that our assemblies, our processes, our concerns and our projects are the democratic ones. And this messy, slow, loud process is exactly what it's going to take to bring peace, justice and joy to our societies.

The recognition that our messiness is a manifestation of democracy is the necessary context for examining controversies within the movement.

11 | Ya basta! We are not only for, we are also against

The term 'anti-globalization' is hotly contested – at least in the Global North. It has become a truism accepted by many movement insiders that the anti-globalization movement is poorly named (in English). Many commentators, in and outside the movement, have argued against the term, some claiming that it was not organically generated. Insiders often claim 'we are not really against globalization':

> The phrase 'anti-globalization' movement is a coinage of the US media and activists have never felt comfortable with it.[1]

> This is why it is not useful to use the language of anti-globalization. Most people do not really know what globalization is, and the term makes the movement extremely vulnerable to stock dismissals like: 'If you are against trade and globalization why do you drink coffee?' Whereas in reality the movement is a rejection of what is being bundled along with trade and so-called globalization.[2]

> This movement, the most globalized in history, which was labeled 'antiglobalization'.[3]

There seem to be several things at issue. First, the term states what the movement is against, but not what it is for. This is seen as weak 'messaging' because it fails to convey clarity about alternatives. A second, related, issue is that it is a 'negative' rather than 'positive' term, causing vision and energy problems of grave concern to some spiritually-grounded activists: 'Every beginning Witch learns that you can't cast a spell for what you don't want.'[4] Third, it implies that the movement is entirely against every kind of global integration.

These naming problems hinge on the conflicting meanings attributed to globalization. For the most part, within the

11 upper: Indymedia Argentina (<argentina.
indymedia.org>)   lower: Jubilee South march
during the World Social Forum in Porto Alegre,
Brazil. 2002 (photo by Tim Russo)

movement 'globalization' is used as a shorthand for what is more precisely named 'corporate globalization', 'corporate colonialism', 'capitalist globalization' or 'the latest phase of colonialism or imperialism', in which global markets, international financial institutions and trade agreements are used by transnational corporations to leverage control over economies at every scale as well as over government policy-making and enforcement.

This process includes the mystification of its own structure and goals through self-characterizations such as 'increased consumer choice', 'technology that brings us all closer', 'feeding the world', poverty alleviation, 'improved international standards' and cultural sharing in the 'global village'. These mass-marketed concepts draw on human strivings and collective activities which have accompanied *and disrupted* colonialism and imperialism at every turn and which long pre-date the project of convincing people that corporate monopolies were desirable, unavoidable and part of the natural evolutionary progress of human beings. (Just as sex is used to sell products in a false promise, family, multiculturalism and women's liberation are used to sell globalization.)

Since the anti-globalization movement promotes international human rights standards (perhaps improved), ending poverty, increased international communication, sharing of ideas and multiculturalism, it seems awkward to oppose their thieving standard-bearer.

Given this mess, there are two strategic choices. One is to reject the process of globalization, revealing its characterizations as stolen and manipulative. The second is to marginalize the corporate meanings of the word and claim 'globalization' as the rightful property of ancient non-capitalist social processes which pre-date it and are wholly independent of it.

In practice, activists have worked with the following concepts:

- We are against colonialism, imperialism, and corporate projects.[5] This 'negative' creates an invaluable positive, one which indeed brought the movement into being – the mutual recognition by diverse movements of a shared enemy. 'With the movement against a monolithic world economic system, people can once again see the enemy more clearly.'[6] This recognition and identification keeps bringing to life new networks, such as Our World is not for Sale.[7] Korean social movements designated 30 October to 14 November 2004 for 'concentrated joint struggles against the specific policies and *globalization in general*'.[8]

We have to start aiming at the head; we have been militants fighting against nuclear power, against homelessness, sexism – different tentacles of the monster ... you really have to aim at the head.[9]

We are not here to debate privatization, or find some 'third way' to finesse it. Everyone here has decided that privatization is bad, and wants to do something to fight it.[10]

But people know what they don't want, and that's a good sign.[11]

The assertion 'Ya basta!' (Enough!) is our first and fundamental point of unity, the 'one no' that precedes our 'many yeses'.

- No matter what language we use, there is no doubt that we know what we are against and that we are also positively and actively creating alternatives. Since the emergence of the World Social Forum, charges that the movement is 'negative' are baseless. 'Our side has always been criticized for only opposing and not proposing. Well, that is no longer valid – if it ever was ... In fact, we feel that many or most of the basic or broad principles for an alternative order are already with us.'[12]

- Our globalization is different. Many activists argue that the movement represents genuine globalization, one which is decentralized, secure, diverse, creative, autonomous, participatory, direct and joyful.

- 'Positive' names have been developed. These include

'globalization from below', 'global justice', 'another world is possible', and, perhaps the best, the French *'altermondialisation'* – which can, if absolutely necessary, be anglicized to 'alterglobalization'. The prefix 'alter' connotes at once both a negative and an alternative. The rest of this book will experiment with this term.

- And a sense of humour! When Ernesto Zedillo described critics as *'globalifobicos'*, Mexican activists embraced the concept and a number of groups formed using the name![13] In 1998 the Zapatistas popularized and PGA adopted the slogan 'First World? Ha! Ha! Ha!', inspiring actions which take the form of laughing at the World Bank (or some other noxious institution) all day.

Notes

1 David Graeber, 'The New Anarchists', pp. 202–15 in Tom Mertes (ed.), *A Movement of Movements: Is Another World Really Possible?* (London: Verso, 2004).

2 Naomi Klein, 'Reclaiming the Commons', *New Left Review*, 9 (May–June 2001).

3 Notes from Nowhere (ed.), 'Walking: We Ask Questions'; *We are Everywhere* (London: Verso, 2003), p. 506.

4 Starhawk, 'Québec City: Beyond Violence and Nonviolence', April 2001, at <www.starhawk.org>

5 James Petras, 'Imperialism and Resistance in Latin America', 6 November 2003.

6 José Bové, 'A Farmers' International' (November 2001), pp. 137–51 in Tom Mertes (ed.), *A Movement of Movements: Is Another World Really Possible?* (London: Verso, 2004).

7 <www.ourworldisnotforsale.org>

8 Korean People's Action against FTAs and WTO (KoPA), 'News Alert #1: Korean Social Movements Prepare for a Series of Joint Struggles Against Neoliberal Globalization', 29 October 2004. <www.antiwto.jinbo.net>

9 Olivier de Marcellus at the founding conference of Peoples' Global Action (1998) in Notes from Nowhere (ed), *We are Everywhere*, p. 101.

Ya basta!

10 Trevor Ngwane, 'Sparks in the Township' (July 2003), pp. 111–34 in Mertes (ed.), *A Movement of Movements*.

11 José Bové in José Bové and François Dufour with Gilles Luneau, *The World is not for Sale: Farmers Against Junk Food*, trans. Anna de Casparis (London: Verso, 2002) pp. 185–8.

12 Walden Bello and Nicola Bullard, 'The Global Conjuncture: Characteristics and Challenges', National Convention Against Globalization, New Delhi, India, 21–23 March 2001.

13 'Ernesto Zedillo Ponce de León' (9 December 2003), in *Wikipedia: The Free Encyclopedia* (it's also participatory). <www.en.wikipedia.org/wiki/Ernesto_Zedillo_Ponce_de_Leon>

12 | Back in black: anarchism and autonomy

In many parts of the world, anarchists have been active in alterglobalization movements. They are grudgingly received by other sectors, who downplay their presence and sometimes actively exclude them. Intense fear of anarchists is rooted in centuries of vilification by capitalists and revolutionary sectors alike. Ridicule and slander of anarchists has even been absorbed into popular culture and dictionaries.

Anarchism is an old Western philosophy dated to Greek Stoics and Cynics, the Diggers and Levellers of the English Revolution,[1] and mid-1800s French and Russian philosopher/revolutionaries.[2] The Second International expelled anarchists in 1896, and they have since been excluded (and alienated) from socialist thought, debate and organizing, although they have also been a constant presence in Western politics.[3]

> For anarchists, anarchy means '*not necessarily absence of order, as is generally supposed, but an absence of rule*' ... For this reason, rather than being purely anti-government or anti-state, anarchism is primarily a movement against *hierarchy*. Why? Because hierarchy is the organisational structure that embodies authority. Since the state is the 'highest' form of hierarchy, anarchists are, by definition, anti-state; but this is *not* a sufficient definition of anarchism ... this opposition to hierarchy ... includes all authoritarian economic and social relationships as well as political ones ... And, just to state the obvious, anarchy does not mean chaos nor do anarchists seek to create chaos or disorder. Instead, we wish to create a society based upon individual freedom and voluntary co-operation. In other words, order from the bottom up, not disorder imposed from the top down by authorities.[4]

Beyond this basic idea, anarchists have worked out a variety

12 Zapatista women in Amador Hernadez demand, daily for more than a year, that the Mexican military leave the village's communal landholdings (photo by Tim Russo)

of different approaches such as primitivism, green anarchism, anarcho-syndicalism, anarchist federalism, anarcho-pacifism, anarcha-feminism and 'anarchism without adjectives'. Rather than signifying mutually exclusive disagreements and contestation, these different names highlight aspects of anarchist theory. Regarding anarchist practice, in building and participating in organizations anarchists strive for

> commitment to confederalism, decentralisation, self-management and decision making from the bottom up. In such organisations the membership play the decisive role in running them and ensuring that power remains in their hands. They express the anarchist vision of the power and creative efficacy people have when they are self-reliant ... Anarchists insist that people must manage their own affairs (individually and collectively) and have both the right and the ability to do so.[5]

Since the recent wave of resistance to globalization, Northern anarchists have noticed that indigenous and Third World communities asserting 'autonomy' are often articulating decentralization, mutual aid and direct democracy. At the same time, forms of autonomy have emerged in the Global North without being anarchist.

These parallel developments have made possible the development of international networks such as Peoples' Global Action, which includes anarchists but is led by non-anarchist autonomous movements, largely from the Global South. Anarchist principles and organizing strategies are widely used in the alterglobalization movement, without formal recognition that these are anarchist concepts and by groups which are not otherwise affiliated with anarchism. A statement from the World Social Forum expresses the omnipresent character of this perspective: 'social hierarchies ... are not a legitimate form of organizing social and economic production and reproduction'.[6] ' ... its decentralized form, its strong anti-bureaucratic impulses and its working through of the ideas of direct democracy, in the spirit of Rousseau – whether one labels that anarchism or not'.[7]

Tute Bianche, 'A Busload of Lies Exposed', July 2001

By the way, why are we not anarchists ourselves?

And why don't we even call ourselves 'communists' any more?

As far as the practical critique to hierarchies and authoritarianism is concerned, we don't have any catching up to do. The fact that we don't call ourselves 'anarchists' stems both from the history and the present of the European far left, whose most advanced and intelligent currents have long bridged the gap between 'socialists', 'communists' and 'anarchists' ...

There's a long tradition of anti-authoritarian communists who antagonized Stalinism, the Soviet Union and the party-form itself ... Several decades later, in the 1970s, Italy became a social laboratory for so-called 'autonomous marxism', a current that advocated the refusal of work and the complete political autonomy of the working class, re-defining the way the working class is perceived, cutting loose from the 2nd, 3rd and 4th Internationals at once. This heterogeneous network had a great influence on social movements, counterculture and the squatters' scene, holding a position traditionally occupied by anarchists in other countries. Even the approach to cyberpunk and net-culture ... wildly horizontal and spontaneous ... moved farther beyond any neat label and description, as Ya Basta! is doing now.

Our theoretical approach still derives from Karl Marx's *Grundrisse* and the texts of 'autonomous' thinkers like Toni Negri (and the notion of 'cultural hegemony' devised by Antonio Gramsci seventy years ago), at the same time, we are beyond all that and have a clear Zapatista influence in the way we speak, organize and take action.

Source: <www.nadir.org/nadir/initiativ/agp/free/genova/busload.html>

The rest of this chapter reviews those anarchist concepts and practices which are in popular use in the alterglobalization movement.

Free association and mutual aid

In 1902, Peter Kropotkin proved, using biological and sociological evidence, that cooperation is more effective than coercion in ensuring survival.[8] Anarchists confidently assert that people will organize themselves to solve community problems, citing the activities of communities throughout human history as evidence.[9] Anything that needs to be analysed, built or resolved can be addressed through mutual aid. People who are most motivated to work on an issue are the best ones to get involved. People will also figure out whom they can work well with. The most efficient and happy group to work in is one which people have freely joined.

Anti-hierarchical practices

Consistent with the critique of rule, anarchists strive in political organizing not to permit any kind of hierarchy to emerge. This leads to rigorous distinctions between hierarchy and authoritative expertise, leadership, facilitation and other moments of non-horizontality, which are often temporary or sharply constrained. In pursuit of non-hierarchy and inclusion, anarchists and other autonomists often use consensus or some other direct democratic practice for making decisions.

There is also a recognition that much can get done without a group decision, through decentralized initiatives and free association. Hence Critical Mass's use of the 'xerocracy' system, in which people spontaneously distribute proposals and those who are interested investigate or advance them further. Such practices are driven in part by avoidance of *unnecessary* decisions, which are understood to indicate a surfeit of power.

In order to prevent or disrupt the emergence and entrenchment of elites, groups emphasize the 'process' of developing people's skills and enthusiasm over the immediate 'product' of a campaign or action. This perspective has been popular in many non-anarchist movements. 'A revolutionary organisation must always remember that its objective is not getting people to listen to speeches by expert leaders, but getting them to speak for themselves.'[10]

DIY

Self-provisioning in daily life is a liberating process which makes autonomy possible on a material level. It demonstrates to participants and observers that ordinary people have the knowledge, skills and communal spirit necessary to rebuild the world.

> Anarchism is all about 'do it yourself', people helping each other out in order to secure a good society to live within and to protect, extend and enrich their personal freedom ... Only by creating practical alternatives can we show that anarchism is a viable possibility and train ourselves in the techniques and responsibilities of freedom ... By building the new world in the shell of the old, we ... create 'schools of anarchism' which lay the foundations for a better society as well as promoting and supporting social struggle against the current system.[11]

This 'prefigurative'[12] action, 'building the new world in the shell of the old', means creating local institutions to meet communal needs. These include social centres, housing, childcare centres, libraries, technology centres, infoshops, meals, craft production, clinics, media production and so forth. The French farmers' movement, Confédération Paysanne, tries to '"change politics gently" by putting their beliefs into practice. "We try not to work too hard, so that others can have work."'[13]

DIY is visible at alterglobalization events where activists themselves spontaneously organize needed services (housing, food, medical care, legal support, education, graphics, media), often through salvaging underused resources.

Worker self-management

When workers take over factories, they are able to determine what is produced, whom production will serve, the quality and quantity of employment, the use to which profit is put, and the social relations of production.[14] These developments are possible and helpful in the course of national struggles[15] or independent from them. The success of worker self-management in widespread experiments is an important demonstration of the viability of anarchist concepts of community self-determination, -organization and -provisioning.

Autonomous zones

Autonomous zones have developed spontaneously without either ideology or anarchists at rock concerts, in neighbourhoods, among artistic communities and as a form of political articulation of indigenous communities. They are temporary spaces of community self-determination which ward off for some period of time commodification and external governance. Anarchists also have a tradition of creating and politicizing such zones. Controversial anarchist author Hakim Bey wrote about them in 1985, hardly interfering at all with their widespread development and practice by non-anarchist autonomists.

> We are creating spaces where people can make their own decisions and can live the way they want to live. You get the same idea in many different countries and places: movements which are organized in horizontal ways, as we are, or whatever other means they are using. I think that we are all working towards the same goal, even if we don't have the same strategy and disagree on certain issues. I think that we have that in common: the idea to create a world where you can decide by yourself ... Building a world beyond capitalism always means confronting capitalism ... They cannot afford to let us escape and build autonomous spaces, because they live on our work, our energy.[16]

According to George Katsiaficas, autonomous movements in European cities during the 1970s and 1980s were not necessarily anarchist. The autonomous zones expressed a political culture of 'immediate activism' in which housing, social

The Village Charter

Preamble: This year, in Evian, the G8 nations summit will take place from the 1st to the 3rd of June 2003. The G8 nations are formed by 8 Northern men who take informal, antidemocratic decisions, who implement warlike and market globalization, who adopt policies disregarding environment, and whose domination exacerbates inequalities and all forms of discrimination. We are strongly opposed to that ... we also have alternative ways of life to put forward. The intergalactic village is the opportunity for us to put them in practice.

Here are these principles: self-management, ecomanagement, the refusal of all sexist, patriarchal, racist, anti-Semite, homophobic, and aggressive behaviour ... turn the village into something more than just a campsite full of individualistic consumers, that is to say into a genuine place of communal life, of exchanges and solidarity at odds with what Evian is going to become.

1) About self-management: The management of the village is a collective one. Each one is part of the decision-making. Each one is responsible for its functioning ... the village is divided into several barrios according to geographical, thematic, political affinities. You can join the barrio of your choice. Each barrio is a self-managed place where you can find a cafeteria and specific activities. Each barrio works as a General Meeting during which the management of collective organizational tasks (cooking, toilets...), the preparation of actions, and the settlement of possible problems are decided. All the village residents are asked to participate in the management of his/her own barrio ... the tasks are shared out ... at odds with all kind of discriminations which traditionally rule in this matter. <g8illegal.lautre.net>

centres and entire districts were squatted, transformed and defended. These movements were antifascist, anti-imperialist, anti-militarist and socialist, but they sought more than 'freedom from material want'. They set about creating a fully-housed society free of the hegemonies of family, state, nuclear power and the Protestant ethic. They fought 'the colonization of everyday life' by asserting freedoms in the realm of family, gender and culture. 'It's not enough to talk. Love is a battle. We are fighting homelessness and gentrification, but also the USA, South Africa, and capitalism to show our solidarity.'[17]

Autonomous temporary villages and other spaces are commonly created as part of the support for large protests and manifestations in the Global North. These spaces often use anarchist organizing principles. The villages are playful and painstaking attempts to establish cooperative political units in the interstices of Global North excess. Even though temporary, they provide a visionary training ground and space of experimentation for alternative political structures.

The Global North experiments are entirely outflanked by the Zapatista movement, which has developed autonomous, indigenous control over healthcare, education, economics, politics, 'defense of language and cultural traditions' and information ('news in local language ... transmitted through the various Zapatista radio stations') within liberated municipalities. In August 2003, regional structures (Good Government Juntas, in five regional Caracoles) were established for the few functions that go beyond the autonomous councils of the local municipalities.[18]

And the Zapatistas are far from the only practical models of autonomy. The Movimento dos Trabajadores Rurais Sem Terra, the movement of landless workers in Brazil, occupies unused lands and establishes autonomous education, provisioning (through production cooperatives) and governance, a model proliferating in Latin America and Africa. As discussed earlier, the *piqueteros* and *asembleas* of Argentina have established, through direct democratic organizing, autonomous neighbourhoods as well as DIY provisioning.

Empirical documentation of the practices of alterglobaliza-tion movements anywhere in the world reveals with surprising consistency assertions of autonomy, practices that decentralize power and production, respect for diversity, and processes of empowerment through participatory, self-reliant and collective problem-solving. These efforts, though diverse and dispersed, are already demonstrating alternative forms of power and that 'Another World is Possible'.

Resources

Anarchism Anarchist FAQ: <www.nadir.org/nadir/initiativ/agp/free/imf/argentina>

CrimethInc. Publications: <www.crimethinc.com>

Anarcho-Syndicalism 101: <www.anarchosyndicalism.org>

A-Infos (multilingual news service by, for and about anarchists): <www.ainfos.ca>

Anarchy Archives: <www.dwardmac.pitzer.edu/anarchist_archives>

Albert Meltzer, *Anarchism: Arguments For and Against* (Oakland, CA: AK Press, 1996).

Dark Star (ed.), *Quiet Rumours: An Anarcha-Feminist Reader* (Oakland, CA: AK Press, 2002).

Zapatistas in Cyberspace: <www.eco.utexas.edu/Homepages/Faculty/Cleaver/zapsincyber.html>

Critical Mass: <www.critical-mass.org>

DIY: George McKay (ed.), *DiY Culture: Party and Protest in Nineties Britain* (London: Verso, 1998).

Stephen Duncombe, *Notes from Underground: Zines and the Politicsof Alternative Culture* (London: Verso, 1997).

Autonomous zones: Movimento de Trabalhadores Rurais Sem Terra: <www.mstbrazil.org>

Sue Branford and Jan Rocha, *Cutting the Wire: The Story of the Landless Movement of Brazil* (London: Latin American Bureau, 2002).

Notes

1 'Gerrard Winstanley ... founded the tiny Digger movement. In his 1649 pamphlet, "Truth Lifting Up Its Head Above Scandals", he wrote that power corrupts, that property is incompatible with freedom, and that men can only be free and happy in a society without governmental interference, where work and its

products are shared' (Brian Crabtree, *The History of Anarchism*, 1992 <www.spunk.org/library/intro/sp000282.txt>).

2 Proudhon: French author of *What is Property?*, 1840, and promoter of federation of autonomous communes; Bakunin: Russian co-founder of the First International, 1863, promoter of 'collectivism' in ownership of means of production; and Kropotkin: Russian promoter of collective ownership of products and the means of production, which ought to be decentralized.

3 Anarchists were powerful in the Russian, French, Spanish and Chinese (see Arif Dirlik, *Anarchism in the Chinese Revolution* [Berkeley: University of California Press, 1991]) revolutions. Anarchists were active in Italy, Australia, Peru, Norway and the USA from the late 1800s and in Korea, Japan, Chile, Peru, Argentina, Poland and Venezuela from the early 1900s. Anarchist concepts were popular among artists and intellectuals in Europe and the USA from the late 1800s on.

4 Anarchist FAQ section A1.1 at <www.anarchismfaq.org>

5 Anarchist FAQ section J3, 'What kinds of organisation do anarchists build?' at ibid.

6 William Fisher and Thomas Ponniah (eds), *Another World is Possible: Popular Alternatives to Globalization at the World Social Forum* (London: Zed Books, 2003), p. 193.

7 Walden Bello, 'The Global South' (July 2002), pp. 49–69 in Tom Mertes (ed.), *A Movement of Movements: Is Another World Really Possible?* (London: Verso, 2004), p. 69.

8 Peter Kropotkin, *Mutual Aid: A Factor in Evolution*, 1902, online at <www.dwardmac.pitzer.edu/Anarchist_Archives/kropotkin/mutaidcontents.html>

9 Colin Ward, *Anarchy in Action* (London: Allen and Unwin, 1973).

10 Guy Debord, quoted in Anarchist FAQ section J3, see note 5.

11 Anarchist FAQ section J5, 'What alternative social organisations do anarchists create?' at <www.anarchismfaq.org>

12 'The embodiment, within the ongoing political practice of a movement, of those forms of social relations, decision-making, culture, and human experience that are the ultimate goal. Developing mainly outside Marxism, it produced a critique of bureaucratic domination and a vision of revolutionary democracy that Marxism generally lacked.' Prefigurative forms of struggle 'permit the masses to define the revolutionary process' and to

125

engage in 'cultural transformation' and the transformation of 'everyday life' (Carl Boggs, 'Marxism, Prefigurative Communism, and the Problem of Workers' Control', *Radical America*, 11, 6–12, 1 [November 1977–February 1978], pp. 99–122). For historical discussions of the stakes of prefiguration, see Barbara Epstein, 'The Politics of Prefigurative Community: The Non Violent Direct Action Movement', in M. Davis and M. Sprinker (eds), *The Year Left*. Vol. 3 of *Reshaping the U.S. Left: Popular Struggles in the 1980s* (London: Verso, 1987).

13 José Bové and François Dufour with Gilles Luneau, *The World is not for Sale: Farmers Against Junk Food*, trans. Anna de Casparis (London: Verso, 2002), p. 173.

14 James Petras and Henry Veltmeyer, 'Worker Self-management in Historical Perspective', *Rebelión*, 25 September 2002.

15 National experiences with worker self-management have been effective in Yugoslavia (1950s), Chile (1970s), Bolivia (1950s), Spain (1930s), Russia (1917–), Italy (1901–), Ukraine (1920s) and Peru (late 1960s). More recently, WSM has been crucial in the recovery of the Argentinian economy. See Scott Rittenhouse, 'A brief history of worker self-management' at <www.anarchosyndicalism.org/articles/sr1.htm>

16 Ezequiel Adamovsky in openDemocracy, 'What is the point of Porto Alegre? Activists from two generations in dialogue', 21 January 2003 at <www.opendemocracy.net>

17 Activist in a 'cop-free zone', Copenhagen, 1986, in George Katsiaficas, *The Subversion of Politics: European Autonomous Social Movements and the Decolonization of Everyday Life* (New Jersey: Humanities Press, 1997).

18 Subcomandante Insurgente Marcos, 'Chiapas: The Thirteenth Stele. Part Five: A History', July 2003. Zapatista communiqués at <www.ezln.org/documentos>

13 | Violence: spikey vs. fluffy

Scholars of social movements generally acknowledge that the use of violence in modern societies increases the chance of success of the overall movement. They also observe that its use by movements varies in direct proportion to the degree of police repression they face. Scholar Donatella della Porta defines political violence as 'collective action that involved physical force, considered at that time as illegitimate in the dominant culture'.[1] Violence, then, is a socially constructed concept, varying from culture to culture and changing over time.

Actions described as 'violent'

A number of different types of actions are at different times construed as 'violent'. This chapter leaves aside all property destruction, which is discussed in a chapter in Part Four, 'Tactics'.

Wearing a mask This is clearly not violence; however, it is often portrayed as prefiguring violent acts. Activists wear masks at protests for reasons to do with security and as a form of solidarity, either with people whose civil and human rights are routinely violated – fellow activists who are *never* safe showing their faces – or with the Zapatistas, who announced themselves internationally as 'The voice that arms itself to be heard. The face that hides itself to be seen.'[2] A Black Bloc activist explains another reason for masking:

> we do not believe in this struggle for the advancement of any one individual. We don't want stars or spokespeople. I think the anonymity of the Black Bloc is in part a response to the problems that young activists see when we look back at the civil rights, anti-war, feminist and anti-nuclear movements. Dependence on charismatic leaders has not only led to

13 upper: In Miami for the FTAA protests in November 2003, forty police agencies terrorized dissenters in what was called a 'model for security' (photo by Tim Russo) lower: Massacre Eldorado dos Carajá-Pará, 1996 (photo by J. Ripper for Movimento dos Trabalhadores Rurais Sem Terra, Brasil)

infighting and hierarchy within the left, but has given the FBI and police easy targets who, if killed or arrested, leave their movements without direction.[3]

Mobile defence Militants are celebrated and welcomed for building barricades or putting their own bodies in the way to protect fellow activists from imminent police attack.

Throwing back tear-gas canisters Although throwing something at the police would satisfy some definitions of offensive violence against persons, activists see this as defensive community service. Activists grab the canisters as quickly as possible and hurl them back. (Please wear protective gloves as the exploding canisters can cause serious burns.) The impact danger of the returned projectiles is minimized by police (and their horses') helmets and body armour.

'Unarresting' During detentions and arrests, militants will mount a distraction of some kind nearby in the hope that the police will have to loosen their grip on the arrestee, who then escapes. Unarresting is particularly important when the arrestee is being beaten, has been selected and targeted by police, or faces particular legal or incarceration risks (people of colour, immigrants, transgender people).

Throwing a doughnut, teddy bear or plastic water bottle at police in riot gear Again, these projectiles may technically satisfy some definitions of offence. However, they pose very little risk of injury. These actions are often pre-meditated acts of humour.

Throwing your empty beer or wine bottle at forces who have been occupying your neighbourhood for several days Not having agreed to any 'action guidelines', local residents sometimes create an air of general insurrection.

Attempting to cross police lines, using cardboard shields, mattresses, long poles, oversized beach balls as defence This tactic will be discussed fully in Chapter 25 on the Tute Bianche.

It does involve hand-to-hand combat with police, but with a spectacular mismatch in weaponry and protection. This combat is effective mostly in affording protection to large groups of activists. It has also resulted in several successful breaches of barricades at elite meetings.

Home-made weapons There has not been a single case of weapons preparation or use by US anti-globalization activists,[4] whose European and Canadian counterparts do occasionally carry Molotov cocktails and similar weapons. Weapons such as knives or guns are not carried by Global North protesters, but rocks and paving stones are sometimes dug up and thrown at police. This is a normal part of European protest, not unique to the alterglobalization movement. In the Global South, protesters are sometimes armed, again primarily with home-made or at-hand weapons such as stones, sticks, machetes or even, in the case of Bolivia, miners' dynamite. Nevertheless, the protesters take most of the casualties.

The only movement strongly associated with anti-globalization[5] which carries firearms is the EZLN (Ejército Zapatista de Liberación Nacional), and they haven't fired a shot since 1994. After consulting with civil society, the Zapatistas use only non-violent methods of political struggle (although they maintain an army and weapons for defence): 'I see our weapons as almost being tokenistic, symbolic – it illustrates the depth of our discontent ... But come on – a stone against a helicopter, a stick against an armoured car – and they call us violent? To be honest, there is no comparison.'[6]

'Day of Our Rage'/General Insurrection In Genoa for the G8 meetings in 2001, the response to police attack of all the mobilizations, regardless of their intentions or permits, led to a general insurrection in which 'members of reformist organizations and parties who got outraged by the police violence ... chose to respond in the best possible way ... This resulted in the most organised riot ... there were people at the front with shields, gloves and masks ... taking care of the tear gas,

and behind them loads of people with rocks and some petrol bombs ... formed barricades which were carried forward every time the cops retreated.'[7] The fact that this insurrection was so broadly joined and went beyond any organization is 'a fact that many people have an interest in concealing'.[8] Activists valorized insurrection as a tactic.

> It is difficult not to feel hatred and bitterness when you ... realise that you, your families, your friends and the people around you, all these lives are geared towards serving the interests of someone else ... I came to Genoa to feel that solidarity, that warmth of people like me and I also wanted some outlet for my anger, and they as the most powerful politicians in the world seemed a justifiable target.[9]

> Because it was a G8 summit, all the world's media were there, and the news and the images of the rioting will have been carried back to almost every country in the world ... It is very valuable for [people in the Global South] to be able to see images of things they are familiar with – poor people fighting the police – taking place in the 'rich' West ... maybe there are people like them in the West fighting for the same things they are fighting for ... The riots in Genoa will send a message of hope to people all over the world.[10]

Police riot The vast preponderance of the violence that occurs at protests is perpetrated by the police. Weapons used in police riots include striking weapons, chemical weapons, electric weapons, projectiles, water cannons and stun grenades. The purportedly 'less lethal' weapons are often used counter to the instructions, as has been revealed in the civil suits in Seattle. An informative report for the European Parliament, presented in 1998, made a 'scientific and technological options assessment' for 'political control'.[11] Police response to European protests included the first use in Sweden of live ammunition against protesters since 1931, occurring in Gothenburg at the EU Summit (15 June 2001). Only a month later, at the G8 meetings in Genoa, police brutally raided a sleeping place (lining people up against the walls and beating them) and fatally shot a protester, Carlo Giuliani.

And that was the status *before* 9/11. After 9/11, harassment, surveillance and sentences increased against anti-globalization activists who were suddenly associated with terrorism either through dramatic and bizarre reclassification of sabotage and property crime or through the purported discovery that protest events were choice platforms for terrorist attacks. Two years after 9/11, the Seattle coalition of unions, anti-poverty groups, environmentalists and students gathered to oppose the FTAA meetings in Miami. No fewer than forty law-enforcement agencies, seven of which were federal, violated protesters' rights – even targeting elders and those attending permitted and educational events. The policing plan was to 'limit' protest in order to 'prevent violence'. In practice, unidentified agents not only prevented limited and disrupted constitutionally protected speech and assembly, but also created a 'deliberate and pervasive pattern of intimidation'[12] including 'hunting'[13] activists violently and indiscriminately for over thirty blocks from the actual meeting site. This police operation seemed intended to terrorize citizens (both participants and observers) from taking part in any future acts of dissent. It was called by Miami authorities a 'model for security'.

> It is a ridiculous presumption in a way to believe that we can 'decide' how the police will react to us. We had ensured we were going to get a violent response by gathering in the streets in such large numbers and announcing our intention to get inside ... This is a provocative and confrontational stance to take, whether or not you are throwing molotov cocktails. The police respond to the level of violence you threaten and to your effectiveness. If you are ineffective but violent, you will probably get a response from the police, if you are ineffective and non-violent then you will probably not get much response from the police, but if you begin to be effective, whether you are using violence or not, then you will be met with a violent response.[14]

This becomes increasingly clear when permitted, pacifist demos are attacked, as they regularly are in the Global South, and increasingly in the Global North.

In the USA, accusing protesters of 'violence' is enough to turn public opinion against them. In contrast, European governments have little space to rationalize their policing or to blame the protesters. The acute historical memory of fascism and nationalist repression are near at hand and easily connected with the imposition of globalization. The murder of Carlo Giuliani was promptly described as assassination.

> ... and young people are shot dead for daring to think there can be another way. The message from the world's authorities is clear: go back to your homes, do not meddle in what doesn't concern you, return to your televisions, to smoking dope and stealing traffic cones and leave the intricacies of global economics alone – because if you don't we will kill you.[15]

Not uncommonly, such attacks are pre-emptive, such as the beating of activists in their sleeping place in Genoa.[16]

Quietly, many activists recognize that experiencing, witnessing, or watching media coverage of arbitrary police violence crystallizes issues of power, order and discipline, with reliably radicalizing effects. 'We left our copy of the European Convention on Human Rights behind agreeing that a lemon[17] would be more useful.'[18]

Is this a violent social movement?

While indeed 'seen as illegitimate', the tactics used in the movement do not meet the criteria for violent struggle, neither that advocated by revolutionary theorists nor that eschewed by non-violent revolutionaries. Violent revolutions as theorized by Maoism, Leninism and Focoism, require 'a people's army', which is not the strategy of anti-globalization movements. Today's militants even disdain guerrilla vanguardism: 'armed struggle is elitist activity conducted by a small group meeting in secret. This is bullshit – we will all do it for ourselves.'[19]

In current usage, 'pacifist' tactics exclude both offensive and self-defensive violence against persons and property. 'Pacific' events meet the standards of pacifism behaviourally, but may choose that tactic for immediate strategy rather than philosophy. 'Non-violence' eschews offensive violence against persons. The self-defence which is engaged by the movement was not forbidden by Gandhi and Martin Luther King, Jr (although they discouraged it as confusing the message at demos).

The demonization of activists whose only 'violence' is tearing down plastic fencing while wearing a mask tells us less about movement tactics than about 'criminalization', which, as Massimo De Angelis points out, has little to do with the breaking of the law: 'Criminalisation occurs when a wall is successfully built between the movement and the rest of society.' In the effort to delegitimize movements, 'Violence can always be found hidden in methods that do not recognise the ways of official authority.'[20]

Movement discourse on violence

The struggle for hegemony over 'legitimacy' establishes the terrain in which social movements work. The most active contestation is whether any of the movement's activities can be compared with the violence of war, neoliberalism and routine police brutality. Starhawk, an influential North American activist, wrote: 'I can no longer use the same word to describe what I've seen even the most unruly elements of our movement do in actions and what the cops did in Genoa.'[21]

This has led some activist groups to reject the dichotomy of violence/non-violence as part of their tactical analysis. In Europe, the tactical disagreements have been renamed 'spikey vs fluffy' – a lighthearted way of pointing out that the fashion differences are more substantive than the tactical ones.

Massimo De Angelis agrees that 'the rigid contraposition between violence and non-violence belongs in the realm of our opponents'.[22] Contesting those definitions after the May 1998 Geneva WTO protests, 'The convenors replied that they regretted the damage to small shops but that this violence was nothing compared to the violence organized in the WTO building.'[23] Non-hegemonic voices receive 'the mark of being "violent" ... while normalized violence remains invisible.'[24]

Meanwhile, in 2001, Peoples' Global Action changed one of their 'Hallmarks' from 'a call to non-violent civil disobedience' to 'a call to direct action and civil disobedience', removing the term 'non-violent'.

> The problem with the old formulation was first that the word 'Non-violence' has very different meanings in India (where it means respect for life) and in the West (where it means also respect for private property) ... The Latin American organisations had also objected to the term ... 'non-violence' [which] seemed to imply a rejection of huge parts of the history of resistance ... The movements of Ecuador and Bolivia ... have actually been practising civil disobedience ... although they may throw some rocks when the army kills with bullets (as it regularly does). In fact, there was always an understanding in PGA that non-violence ... must always be understood relative to the particular political and cultural situation.[25]

It would, however, be a mistake to associate non-violence with Northern movements and violence with Southern ones. A Southern activist argues that 'Only a non-violent struggle can provide the silence in which the questions we are asking can be heard.'[26]

On a strategic level, some activists believe that any image that can be construed as 'violent' discredits, delegitimizes or distracts from the movement's message. In response, others argue that the media tend not to cover demonstrations *unless they violate what is considered to be legitimate*. Typically, 'The first march ... went off peacefully ... Police were persuaded to back off ... All the various groups marched. There was no trouble and, of course, no coverage in the media.'[27] Militant tactics attract the interest of the mainstream press more consistently than any others (pacifist messages and images are often ignored, regardless of the size of the demo). The movement has not always been successful in connecting militant imagery with substantive messages, often marginalizing

Violence

or trying to distract the media from militant minorities. But even when the movement is neither able to capitalize on nor suppress discourse on militance, it is not insignificant that media coverage of militant actions displaces 'official' news (a project at which pacifist movements are weak).

Despite what seems at times to be vociferous disagreement on terms and tactics, all parties in fact agree to the actual practice of using no violence towards persons. The debates in fact are about property crime, barricade breaking and building, and self-defence. In these discussions, human life is honoured and the working-class background of the police is acknowledged.[28] Moreover, all sectors are willing to collaborate in pacific events when necessary. For example 'the immigrants' march ... was to be entirely peaceful as the immigrants themselves were to be on the march'.[29] Militants 'were happy to stick to that knowing'[30] that the next day was 'the day of reckoning, the day of our rage'[31] in which banks would be burned and attempts made to enter the meetings.

Resources

Mark Juergensmeyer, *Gandhi's Way: A Handbook of Conflict Resolution* (formerly *Fighting with Gandhi*, 1984) Berkeley: University of California Press, 2002).

On Fire: *The Battle of Genoa and the Anti-capitalist Movement* (London: One-off Press, 2001).

Ward Churchill, *Pacifism as Pathology* (1986) (Winnipeg: Arbeiter Ring, 1998).

Notes

1 Donatella della Porta, *Social Movements, Political Violence, and the State* (Cambridge: Cambridge University Press, 1995).

2 Subcomandante Marcos, 'Opening Remarks at the First Intercontinental Encuentro for Humanity and Against Neoliberalism', 27 July 1996, San Andres Sacamch'en de los Pobres, Chiapas, Mexico.

3 Mary Black, 'Letter from Inside the Black Bloc', *AlterNet*, 25 July 2001.

4 At the November 2003 FTAA protests in Miami, the illegal searches were so widespread that the police and public now know

with great certainty that protesters, even the grubbiest, angriest and most vegetarian of them, who were subject to the most profiling and, in many cases, multiple illegal stops and searches during the week, were not found to be carrying a single weapon! These were in fact probably the most upstanding collection of youngsters in the world, since these searches also resulted in only one charge of a controlled substance and it turned out to be a prescription medication! For more on Miami see my 'Hunted in Miami: "The Model for Homeland Defense"', *The Commoner*, 29 November 2003, n. 9.

5 A number of anti-imperialist national liberation movements are also anti-globalization movements.

6 Jazz, 'The Tracks of Our Tears', pp. 80–99, in *On Fire: The Battle of Genoa and the Anti-capitalist Movement* (London: One-off Press, 2001).

7 K, 'Being Black Bloc', pp. 31–5 in ibid., p. 35.

8 Ibid.

9 Diego Jones, 'Shooting Blanks?', pp. 7–15 in ibid., pp. 8–9.

10 Anonymous, 'Being Busy', pp. 41–54 in ibid., p. 50.

11 Directorate General for Research, 'Scientific and Technological Options Assessment: An Appraisal of Technologies of Political Control', European Parliament, Luxembourg, 6 January 1998, at <www.uhuh.com/nwo/europarl.htm>

12 Bentley Killmon et al. v. City of Miami ... Tom Ridge, John Ashcroft et al., Class Action Complaint, US District Court for the Southern District of Florida, Miami Division. Filed 24 March 2004 at <www.stopftaa.org/downloads/killmoncomplaint.pdf>

13 Miami Activist Defense, Press Release, 'Miami Mayor Diaz's "Model for Homeland Defense" Equals Suspension of the Constitution and Brutality for FTAA Dissenters', 26 November 2003, archived at <www.stopftaa.org/legal>

14 Anonymous, 'Being Busy', p. 49.

15 Richard K. Moore, 'Beyond Genoa – Where to Now?', pp. 135–9 in *On Fire*, p. 135.

16 Indymedia Italia, 'Genoa G8: What Happened?', at <italy.indymedia.org/news/2001/07/7517.php>

17 As protection from tear-gas, a damp cloth with lemon or vinegar is held over the nose and mouth.

18 John Hughes, 'Life During Wartime', pp. 23–9 in *On Fire*, p. 25.

19 Jazz, 'The Tracks of Our Tears', pp. 91, 98.

20 Massimo De Angelis, 'From Movement to Society', pp. 109–24 in ibid., p. 117.

21 Starhawk, 'Staying on the Streets', pp. 125–34 in ibid., p. 130.

22 Massimo De Angelis, 'From Movement to Society', pp. 109–24 in ibid., p. 122.

23 *Peoples' Global Action Against 'Free' Trade and the WTO*, 2 (June 1998), at <www.agp.org>

24 De Angelis, 'From Movement to Society', p. 118.

25 Peoples' Global Action, 'Hallmarks', changed at 3rd PGA Conference in Cochabamba, Bolivia, September 2001. <www.nadir.org/nadir/initiativ/agp/free/pga/hallm.htm>

26 Chittaroopa Palit, 'Monsoon Risings: Mega-Dam Resistance in the Narmada Valley' (May 2003), pp. 71–93 in Tom Mertes (ed.), *A Movement of Movements: Is Another World Really Possible?* (London: Verso, 2004), p. 90.

27 Adam Porter, 'It Was Like This Before … ', pp. 75–9 in *On Fire*, p. 75.

28 Hughes, 'Life During Wartime', p. 23.

29 Anonymous, 'Being Busy', p. 43.

30 Ibid.

31 Jazz, 'The Tracks of Our Tears', p. 87.

14 | Consumption politics

In the Global North, consumer awareness is a component of political consciousness. Access to tropical products and inexpensive manufactured goods are understood as everyday manifestations of global or imperial privilege. A number of different kinds of consumer action projects have been developed which seek to change international relations of production and consumption. While similar consciousness and practices certainly exist in the Global South, these practices are not understood as major points of confrontation for Global South movements, as they are in the North.

Self-provisioning

Deep ecology texts such as E. F. Schumacher's 1973 *Small is Beautiful* and Duane Elgin's 1981 *Voluntary Simplicity* encouraged people to find pleasure by living within their economic and ecological means by reducing acquisitions. Practitioners hope cumulatively to reduce pressure on the ecology and to enable Global South peoples to keep their resources for their own use.

Practitioners learn their grandparents' skills: to grow and preserve their own food, to make their own medicine, produce their own household items such as soap and candles, brew beer and fuel, produce their own energy, and build their own houses with recycled and renewable materials. One of the most significant practices is the popular return to seasonal eating and relationships with local farms through farmers' markets and new direct farm-consumer institutions.[1] Refreshing the image of this movement, the culturally savvy Church of Stop Shopping from New York City theatrically 'identifies' evil where it finds sweatshop goods. Reverend Billy of the Church says, 'We don't know how to stop chain stores and globalization. We're figuring it out.'[2]

14 Logo courtesy of Equal Exchange, USA

Self-provisioning uses two distinct strategies to change international relations. First, it reduces to some extent the demand for timber, winter tomatoes, oil and sweatshop goods. Second, it propagates cultural changes in the First World. In some cases, this cultural change proposes that standards of living can be *maintained* using ecologically sound and socially just alternatives. In other cases, perhaps most visible in the community of activist punk rock and street youth, the cultural change is conceptualized as a massive *reduction* in First World standards of living.

Activists who meet their needs through alternatives or reduce their needs in advance of systemic change are practising a form of 'prefigurative' politics, which embody the movement's vision as if it were already achieved, thereby calling it into being. Prefigurative approaches in general are hotly contested, being seen by some as absolutely necessary for integrity of the movement and by others as a privileged distraction from struggle against oppression and injustice.

Boycotts

Boycotts were organized throughout the South African apartheid regime and against other repressive regimes. The first powerful citizen boycott of the anti-corporate era was the 1977–84 INFACT boycott of Nestlé in a successful effort to stop misleading and life-threatening advertising of infant formula in the Third World. These days, numerous boycotts are ongoing and several organizations issue compilation lists. The boycotts range from specific products and corporations to World Bank bonds.

Fair Trade

Beginning in the 1940s, socially concerned firstworlders set up 'alternative trade' schemes with poor communities in the Third World. At first marketing handicrafts and ensuring a good return to artisans, Fair Trade has increasingly turned its attention to mass consumption imports taken for granted by First World consumers (an economic matrix largely intact since colonialism). The scheme of a Fair Trade 'label' for items such as bananas, coffee, tea, cocoa and chocolate was begun in 1988 by a Dutch coffee company. The most impressive gains have been made in the coffee industry, with corporate purveyors now creating extensive demand for Fair Trade supplies. But the concept has been extended into a framework for marketing forest products, the handicrafts of low-income communities of the Global North as well as the South, and apparel. A international bureaucracy of Fair Trade certification organizations has emerged, accompanied by critics of the whole thing who argue that 'consuming justice' sidesteps some of the most important problems.[3]

Local markets

As local markets are annihilated by corporate offensives, activists are increasingly trying to politicize local markets, illustrating their non-economic benefits. The simplest method, and the most widespread, is the resurgence and repopularization of open-air and public markets which provide space for small entrepreneurs and bar large retailers. Public markets allow entrepreneurs to bring their goods to market with little capital, to experiment with products, and to depend on the market's visibility in lieu of advertising.

The most significant sector in which consumption is being transformed by politicizing local markets is the food system – generating models that it is hoped will spread to additional economic sectors.

Community Supported Agriculture (CSA – also known as Subscription Agriculture or Box Schemes) was developed in the late 1960s in Japan under the name 'farming with a face on it'. This new economic institution provides secure income to farmers while linking urban families to the changing fate of the farm, to seasonal food cycles and to agronomy. Families purchase a share of the harvest once a year and receive a weekly basket of whatever is ripe, sharing with the farmer both the bounties and losses of the harvest.[4]

In Europe the Slow Food movement (founded 1986) started

to defend 'the right to taste'.[5] At first, Slow Food facilitated food education with schoolchildren to 'improve knowledge about production processes and establish direct contacts with farmers and artisans'. Then it began to 'defend food heritage' by acting on behalf of disappearing varietals and artisanal products. 'At first sight, such products may appear to be no more than the results of microeconomies, but in actual fact they represent a safety net for the entire European agricultural sector.'[6] The gastronomic end of the movement mobilizes chefs and gourmets around active change in economic institutions and relationships.

As issues of sustainability, food culture and community-based economics have converged, the possibility of local food systems has attracted attention in many sectors. Urban economic policy experiments have included attempts to 'shorten the food links', by bringing farmers and consumers closer together as the beginning of redeveloping the local economy.[7] 'Food circles' aim to develop decentralized and sustainable food systems by linking consumers, farmers, retailers, scholars and environmentalists.[8] These new institutions, alongside traditional farmers' markets, respond to food safety concerns and hunger with direct relationships between consumers and farmers.

The US Community Food Security movement, founded in 1995, works to build 'a more democratic food system' by reconceptualizing the food economy around 'community need'.[9] Activists have challenged the charity approach to hunger, organizing food banks, family farm networks, anti-poverty organizations, community development organizations, farmers' markets and the sustainable agriculture movement around 'the notion that all people should have access to a nutritious diet from ecologically sound, local, non-emergency sources'. New technologies have been developed, such as CSAs redesigned for low-income families who cannot invest up-front in the harvest, farmers' markets for low-income neighbourhoods, urban gardens, community kitchens, incubators for processed food micro-enterprises, baby-food making and other cooking classes, shuttle services to facilitate access to higher-quality and lower-priced grocery stores outside the neighbourhood, and local 'food policy councils' (local bodies that analyse and design interventions into the 'foodshed' and 'foodscape').[10]

Analysis

Consumption politics have a number of benefits. They are excellent educational gateways to political economic questions and issues. For example, educational contact with Fair Trade coffee immediately reveals the huge gap between consumer price and the farmers' price. It demonstrates that alternative economic relationships can significantly increase payments to farmers with negligible impact on consumer price. These lessons inspire further study of international trade relations and economics while demonstrating that alternative economic and social relations are eminently possible. Another significant educational impact is demonstrating the illusion of choice provided by corporations (shoes in many styles, but none made by a union). Panicked shoppers, realizing there is no choice, begin to consider political options. Everyday transactions come into focus, fraught with international injustices.

A second accomplishment is the development of 'cultures of resistance'.[11] The resistance created by consumption politics takes place within the space and concepts of daily life. While 'everyday life' has increasingly become a site for political action,[12] consumption politics create meaningful activity for participants and can be understood as 'practices of commitment' which continually reaffirm values.[13] These countercultural practices may also contribute to the development of alternative identities that support 'cultures of resistance'. Addressing the important place of critical consumption in countercultural identity formation, Maria Mies and Veronika Bennholdt-Thomsen challenge feminists and others not to base their liberation on 'loot' and their identity on 'disgust ... degradation and contempt' for peasants.[14]

The most common debate about consumption politics is whether it is effective. But one must ask 'At doing what?'

- Is it catching on? Well, yes. Participation in Fair Trade, sustainable building, alternative fuels, farmers' markets and other alternative consumption systems is rising steadily, in some sectors at a rate of 20 per cent growth per year.
- Does it help the producers? Alternative and direct marketing schemes are keeping in business small producers for whom the wholesale price is below the cost of production. Nearly a million producer families in the Global South participate in Fair Trade schemes alone. As long as demand holds, it is by far the best option available to them.
- Does it democratize relationships between producer and consumer? An increase in justice is, in part, about material well-being addressed above. The second component of justice is power. Consumption politics leaves the power in the hands of Northern consumers, who may change their minds about integrating their values into their everyday lives if doing so becomes inconvenient, expensive, or stigmatizing. Even the best of these systems still leaves producers dependent on consumer fads and rigid aesthetic requirements – and the decisions of powerful marketeers.
- Does it change or establish new trade patterns? Sometimes. In the case of Fair Trade, the basic orientation of the colonial commodity trading system with powerful Northern middlemen (who happen to be non-profit) and finicky consumers (who happen to want justice in their chocolate) is unchanged. In the case of farmers' markets and other alternative food systems, new and qualitatively different trade relationships are established. In the case of self-production (backyard fuel and household products), commodification itself is being challenged.
- Is it anti-capitalist/anti-systemic? These practices are at once 'in and against' the market;[15] they are reforms.

Each practice which could be categorized as consumption politics is subject to a rich internal discourse about goals, effectiveness and regressive aspects. The most consistent critique is that the overall impact of non-participation in this form is negligible and activists' energies would be better spent in direct confrontation with global economic structures than in removing their few dollars from WalMart, McDonalds and Shell Oil. Of course, the very survival of small producers is at stake in this assessment of where to focus energy.

Even the promising accomplishments of consumption politics in the landscape of identity and culture have unfortunate side-effects. A second theme of critiques is that the practices depend on individualism. As a result they lead to a 'lifestyle' form of activism,[16] which is often contrasted dichotomously with collective action. (It should be pointed out that activists' lives are rarely as dichotomous as their critics' arguments.)

Some anti-consumption countercultures alienate potential sympathizers from the broader society by limiting communication to what appears to be a self-congratulatory clique. The behavioural and stylistic purism of counterculture activists can alienate even fellow activists for whom politicized consumption is impractical or inaccessible.

Meanwhile, greenwashing and other corporate practices coopt radical consumption movements, convincing potential activists that they can indeed shop for a better world. The activity of purifying their homes and bodies from Third World blood and corporate toxins can become a full-time job. The very notion of consumer choice as a space of powerful action implies a very high status in the global hierarchy. Exercising great privilege in this trivial way might seem strange to those for whom new shoes would bring an increment of freedom or credibility.[17] Interestingly, privileged people's voluntary embrace of a lower standard of living is not experienced as solidarity by less privileged folks in their own societies or elsewhere. Instead, the countercultures which result are experienced as new (and odd) iterations of privileged culture which extend elites' righteous monopoly on cultural correctness.

Perhaps consumption activists will bridge the meaningful experiences of consumption politics to more collective and confrontational projects so that Fair Trade will become a gateway drug into a powerful world of ever-more intense and meaningful action.

Resources

Fair trade: David Ransom, *The No-Nonsence Guide to Fair Trade* (London: Verso, 2001).

Gregory Dicum and Nina Luttinger, *The Coffee Book* (New York: New Press, 1999).

Randy Charles Epping, *A Beginner's Guide to the World Economy* (New York: Vintage, 1992).

Fairtrade Labeling Organization (consortium of Fair Trade groups in Japan, Canada, the USA and seventeen European countries) <www.fairtrade.net>

Fair Trade México: <www.comerciojusto.com.mx>

Local markets: Gary Paul Nabhan, *Coming Home to Eat: The Pleasures and Politics of Local Foods* (New York: W. W. Norton, 2002).

Carl Honoré, *In Praise of Slowness: How a Worldwide Movement is Challenging the Cult of Speed* (San Francisco, CA: Harper, 2004).

Slow food: <www.slowfood.com>; <www.openair.org>

Community Food Security Coalition: <www.foodsecurity.org>

Boycotting: Infact: <www.infact.org>

Boycott lists at: <www.boycottnet.org>; <www.ethicalconsumer.org>

Liza Featherstone, *Students Against Sweatshops* (London: Verso, 2002). <www.usasnet.org>

Reduction: The Church of Stop Shopping: <www.revbilly.com>

Notes

1 Community Food Security, Local Food Policy Councils, Community Supported Agriculture, etc. Note that these approaches far surpass the already corporate organic food movements.

2 Play Loud! Productions, *Reverend Billy & the Church of Stop Shopping*, dir. Dietmar Post, 60 minutes, 2002. <www.playloud.org/revbilly.html>

3 Josée Johnston, 'Consuming Social Justice', *Arena Magazine*, 51 (March 2001), pp. 42–7. Aimee Shreck, 'Resistance, Redistribution, and Power in the Fair Trade Banana Initiative', *Agriculture and Human Values*, forthcoming.

4 Trauger Groh and Steven McFadden, *Farms of Tomorrow Revisited: Community Supported Farms – Farm Supported Communities* (1990) (Biodynamic Farming and Gardening Association, 1998). Daniel Imhoff, 'Community Supported Agriculture: Farming with a Face on It', in J. Mander and E. Goldsmith (eds), *The*

Case Against the Global Economy (San Francisco, CA: Sierra Club Books, 1996).

5 John-Thor Dahlburg, 'Cooking Up a Reply to Big Mac: The Slow Food Movement', *Los Angeles Times*, 18 November 1998, pp. A1, A24.

6 Carlo Petrini in *Il Sole 24 Ore*, no date. See <www.slowfood. com>

7 Helena Norberg Hodge at the International Forum on Globalization, Global Teach-in, 3: The Social, Ecological, Cultural and Political Costs of Economic Globalization, Berkeley, CA, 11–13 April 1997. Dave Campbell, 'Community Controlled Economic Development as a Strategic Vision for the Sustainable Agriculture Movement', *American Journal of Alternatives*, 12, 1 (1997), pp. 37–44.

8 Mary K. Hendrickson, *The Kansas City Food Circle: Challenging the Global Food System*, dissertation, 1997, University of Missouri-Columbia.

9 Andy Fisher, co-founder of the Community Food Security Coalition and author of the policy paper that led to the development of the 1996 Congressional Food Security Act. See <www. foodsecurity.org>

10 In 1991 Arthur Getz reconfigured the analytic framework of 'watershed' around the local food system's 'carrying capacity' in order to trace a 'foodshed' ('Urban Foodsheds', *Permaculture Activist*, VII, 3 [1991], pp. 26–7). Kenneth A. Dahlberg, 'Food Policy Councils: The Experience of Five Cities and One County', paper presented to the Joint Meeting of the Agriculture, Food and Human Values Society and the Society for the Study of Food and Society, Tucson, AZ, June 1994. Kenneth A. Dahlberg, Kate Clancy, Robert L. Wilson and Jan O'Donnell, 'Strategies, Policy Approaches, and Resources for Local Food System Planning and Organizing' (Local Food System Project: February 1997) <unix. cc.wmich.edu/~dahlberg/F1.pdf>

11 Cultures of resistance are hybrid cultures explicitly connected to particular struggles and to the activity of social struggle itself. While academics get caught up in obscure discussions about the nature of culture (perhaps *all* culture is resistance … perhaps wearing Nikes and drinking Starbucks Coffee while watching *Baywatch* can be done in a resistive way? …), activists use the term in a grassroots, common sense – cultures of resist-

ance are those which support, encourage and provide tools for explicit political struggle. They often have strong links with traditional or indigenous cultures.

12 Richard Flacks, *Making History: The American Left and the American Mind* (New York: Columbia University Press, 1988). Alberto Melucci, *Nomads of the Present* (Philadelphia, PA: Temple University Press, 1989).

13 Robert N. Bellah et al., *Habits of the Heart: Individualism and Community in American Life* (Berkeley: University of California Press, 1985).

14 Veronika Bennholdt-Thomsen and Maria Mies, *The Subsistence Perspective: Beyond the Globalized Economy* (London: Zed Books, 1999).

15 M. B. Brown, *Fair Trade* (London: Zed Books, 1993).

16 See Murray Bookchin, *Social Anarchism or Lifestyle Anarchism: An Unbridgeable Chasm* (Oakland, CA: AK Press, 1996).

17 For a full discussion of these issues with regard to the US movement, see my 'How Can Anti-Imperialism not be Anti-Racist?', *Journal of World-Systems Research*, X, 1 (Winter 2004) at <www.jwsr.ucr.edu/archive/vol10/number1/pdf/jwsr-v10n1-starr.pdf>

15 Signs asking for 'jobs with justice' being readied
for a march (photo by Tim Russo)

15 | Reformism

Reforms are of concern because they satisfy, confuse, divide or coopt social movements, undermining their momentum by addressing only a piece of the problem. Reforms vary in their degree of genuine usefulness, intentional guile and de-mobilizing effects. Some reforms, such as barring user fees from World Bank-funded health projects, build momentum. Others, such as the HIPC initiative for partial debt relief, are time-consuming roadblocks for movements, which must direct energy into demonstrating the reforms' inadequacy and do so against expensive chicanery.

Anti-reformist critiques are as diverse and confusing as reforms themselves. Some anti-capitalists reject the entire anti-globalization movement as reformist because of its lack of explicit opposition to capitalism. Anti-reformists within the movement often reject other parts of the movement based on their formal character (NGOs), tactics, exclusionary or elitist structures,[1] or inadequately revolutionary rhetoric. Another unfortunate anti-reformist tendency actually opposes any amelioration, fearing the demobilizing effects.

The extremes of both reformism and anti-reformism are unmanned outposts in the anti-globalization movement. Indeed, the movement can be distinguished by its manifestos' uncompromising critiques of capitalism[2] (although the failure to use that word causes much consternation) and simultaneous embrace of participants' autonomously defined struggles. The fiercest anti-reformist rhetoric is inseparable from tremendous mutual respect among grassroots movements for one another's goals and victories. While reformist ideology is roundly rebuked (and NGOs purveying it are bitterly resented), reformist strategy is broadly understood as part of building cultures of resistance through urgent, tangible struggles.

As accusations of reformism are both politically indispensable and treacherously divisive, great care must be exercised both analytically and strategically. To that end, this chapter considers three aspects of reformism in the anti-globalization movement. It does not review the prolific history of relevant debates.

Post-colonial radicalism in the Global South

Since guiding principles of anti-globalization come from the Global South, a clear conception of Global South radicalism and its context is essential to understanding reformist projects in the movement.

In postcolonial nations, the process of de-colonization is far from complete. Colonialism was a brutal process of military and political conquest which also displaced traditional cosmology, jurisprudence, educational systems, healthcare, language and reciprocal economic relations. One of its most devastating legacies, largely unrepaired, is land distribution. While many postcolonial nations have implemented land reform, lack of access to land remains the primary cause of hunger in the Global South.[3]

At its most sophisticated, colonialism also manufactured race, class and gender hierarchies which remain to this day. The cultural, ideological and associated psychological impacts of colonialism continue to shape the definition of dignity throughout the Global South. Decisions about development are taken in a matrix of tension over the personal, social and national value and viability of endogenous technologies and culture.

Operating in this matrix, activists in the Global South are fighting a number of simultaneous but quite different struggles. First, they are dealing with specific local crises caused by corporate projects, increasing inequality, national debt and military imperialism. This means they are fighting the privatization of electricity systems, violations of labour law by multinational corporate sweatshops, evictions, healthcare crises,[4] CIA plots and military action both formal (increasingly in the guise of anti-terrorism or crime fighting) and informal (paramilitary, private security or militarized police).

Second, they are battling the psychological and ideological legacies of colonialism. In dialogue with their fellow citizens, activists challenge hundreds of years of programming that 'West is best', that consumerism is dignity, and that there really is no alternative to the plans of the silver-tongued Northern elites. As part of this work, some radical Global South activists make detailed scholarly analyses of international policy proposals.[5]

The third, and perhaps most familiar, face of Global South struggle is a nationalist response to structural adjustment programmes and free trade agreements. Because these policies result in outside authorities dictating laws and policy in postcolonial nations, they are experienced as 'recolonization'. Resistance takes many forms, from direct action against privatization projects to the assertion of national sovereignty. Although postcolonial nationalism has been oppressive and brutal when it has (often with outside assistance) escaped control of the people, defending national sovereignty means defending many progressive elements of postcolonial states, such as land reform law, nationalization of major industries, public services and welfare programmes.

Regional trading blocs among Global South countries are being organized (most rapidly in Latin America) as a mutual support system to ease the transition from distorted export-dependent economies to production for self-consumption. Such blocs would be a crucial element of a debtors' cartel. As these blocs emerge, activists and movements will have to struggle against regional hegemonies.

Global South nationalism has also provided international leadership on the development of the Biosafety Protocol (since eviscerated by being subjugated to the WTO which prohibits the precautionary principle). This form of postcolonial nationalism profoundly confronts racism, hierarchy and paternalism and embraces humanitarian internationalism through democratic processes independent of G8 rhetoric and elitist manipulation.

The fourth struggle of Global South activists is with their

153

own elites, who often benefit personally from the continued relations of paternalism. Many of these elites have collaborated in the implementation of recolonization. Intermittently, Global South elites are held accountable by social movements and work in solidarity with fellow Global South elites to put the brakes on WTO expansion and new FTAs. But even in the best cases, popular democratic, socialist or humanitarian Global South officials have had little room for manoeuvre under the squeeze of international capital and international financial institutions. This explains the tremendous struggles of the Anti-Privatization Forum and many other South African organizations against the African National Congress (Mandela's party), which is now implementing neoliberalism apace.[6]

While there are commonalities among postcolonial nations, their experience and current conditions vary widely as a result of their specific histories, the successes of internal movements for democratization, their relations with regional and global elites, and a variety of other factors. Competition and tension between postcolonial nations are as common as friendship and solidarity. As a result, the fifth struggle of Global South activists is the effort to develop international solidarity at every possible level, across barriers of language, culture, nationalism, race and class. Activists are bypassing formal national processes to build direct connections among grassroots movements. Vía Campesina is one of the most impressive examples. This work takes many forms, including the difficulty of working with sympathetic but often paternalistic Northern movements.

The project of Vía Campesina to 'remove agriculture from the WTO' appears at first to be quite reformist. It implies a tolerance for a WTO without an agreement on agriculture. It suggests that in the absence of WTO intervention the world food system would be just. Likewise Jubilee (formerly Jubilee 2000) campaigns seem obsessed with Third World debt – implying to some observers the fantasy that postcolonial countries have a chance to be free of imperialism in the context of US militarism and global capitalism if only they didn't have a foreign debt. And the South African Anti-Privatization Forum

(APF) may seem to some to be obsessed with affordable utilities in the context of poverty and devastation which have in many respects increased since the apartheid era.

But Vía, Jubilee and the APF are all comprehensive, aggressive anti-systemic social movements. Their key issues are articulated in terms of life and death for millions of constituents. Their organizing includes all related issues of power and oppression. There is simply no avoiding the fact that, if taken to their conclusion, all of these organizations' policies are anti-capitalist. (For example, Vía Campesina's fundamental policy is 'food sovereignty'.)

Organizations and movements cannot be dismissed as reformist on the basis of one or another policy which they at times promote. Nor can the 'reformist' label be easily attached to the appearance or absence of particular words, as further examination of manifestos reveals anti-imperialist and anti-systemic analysis among organizations that do not immediately present anti-capitalist rhetoric.

Rapidly coalescing solidarity among Global South grassroots movements has produced widely shared perspectives. These include the illegitimacy and outright rejection of the debts of poor countries, the rejection of patents on life, food sovereignty, and the need to reclaim the commons (discussed in Part Two: Manifestos, above).

Another potent issue gaining ground in the Global South is reparations for slavery and colonialism. Not surprisingly, analyses continue to reveal the strength of economic continuities between the colonial era and the current processes of impoverization, imperial projects and ecological rape. The Organization of African Unity sponsored a Commission on Reparations which, along with the Group of Eminent Persons, formulated the Abuja Proclamation in 1993: 'serves notice on all states in Europe and the Americas which had participated in the enslavement and colonisation of the African peoples, and which may still be engaged in racism and neo-colonialism, to desist from any further damage and start building bridges of conciliation [and] co-operation ... through reparation'. At the

**Platform of the International Movement ATTAC,
adopted December 1998**

More generally, the goals are:

• to reconquer space lost by democracy to the sphere
  of finance,
• to oppose any new abandonment of national sovereignty on the pretext of the 'rights' of investors and
  merchants,
• to create a democratic space at the global level.

It is simply a question of taking back, together, the future
of our world.

Source: <www.attac.org>

2001 United Nations World Conference against Racism in Durban,[7] reparations were discussed and integrated with analyses
of the racialized effects of globalization, but not included in
the final declaration. The issue has also since been taken up
by Human Rights Watch, which proposes a 'focus on people
who can reasonably claim that today they personally suffer
the effects of past human rights violations through continuing
economic or social deprivation'.[8]

Reformism as pedagogy

ATTAC, the International Movement for Democratic Control
of Financial Markets and Their Institutions, is often characterized dismissively as aiming only for a small reformist tax on
international speculative transactions (the Tobin Tax).

José Bové argues that what is important about ATTAC is
the 'collective pedagogy'. According to Bernard Cassen, ATTAC
used the Tobin Tax 'as a symbolic terrain on which to raise
questions about the way in which financial markets function'. In his view, ATTAC is an 'action-oriented movement of
popular education', ensuring that militants are 'well-informed,
intellectually equipped for action'. Due to the high 'scientific'

standards of ATTAC's work, 'many ATTAC members know more about the WTO than our parliamentarians'.[9] In 2004, there were chapters of ATTAC in thirty-eight countries, all organized from the grassroots. A multilingual weekly newsletter documents activity on a diverse array of issues with a fully anti-imperialist perspective.

ATTAC's pedagogical use of the Tobin Tax is similar to Oxfam's use of 'wedge issues'.

> A wedge provides a concrete illustration of a problem caused by global policies in a form that can be easily understood by the broader public. The idea is that once people understand the grassroots, human impact of particular policies, they will be encouraged to campaign for broader policy change. So, for example, the problem of patents and access to medicines is a 'wedge' issue for the reform of TRIPS. The fact that no poor country could afford expensive, patented HIV/AIDS medicines provided a particularly dramatic illustration of the problem.
>
> Prior to the launch of Cut the Cost, Oxfam's research showed that few people knew what a patent was, and that if they did know, they were more likely to think that it was a good thing than a bad thing. Even fewer people knew what the WTO or TRIPS were. On the other hand, many more people were concerned about health in poor countries.[10]

Oxfam rejects the binary choice between working for incremental and fundamental change, arguing that seemingly reformist wedge issues can be used to delegitimize the market system. While Oxfam's approach to educational work is a good example of how reformism can be strategic, in 2002 the organization broke solidarity with the anti-globalization movement by issuing a report endorsing free trade as a solution to poverty.[11] The report (controversial even within the organization) is a more sound basis for an accusation of reformism than many.

Pedagogical reformism is a tactic, obsessive criticism of which can only be described as fetishism. The strategy of *specifismo* encourages contextuality in tactics and ideological

157

non-rigidity when participating in larger campaigns, projects or actions.

Monopolize resistance

The World Social Forum has been conceptualized as 'a pedagogical and political space' rather than a 'deliberative body'.[12] Nevertheless, concerns have been raised that some of the conveners are intent upon centralization, control, stardom, bureaucracy, representative or party politics, and moderation. Radical social movements find themselves increasingly uncomfortable, in part because the invitation to 'civil society' seems far too inclusive. 'For example, the mayor of Buenos Aires, Aníbal Ibarra, usually goes to the Forum. He's the guy who we're actually fighting against in the city ... so it feels really annoying that we have to share that space with him.'[13]

Dissenters' activities around the forum have been marginalized and even criminalized by the hosts, who have repeatedly sent in the riot police against would-be WSF participants. At the 2004 meeting in Mumbai a parallel meeting was held called Mumbai Resistance (MR) accusing the WSF of including people who 'only posture as being against globalization'.

> On the contrary, I believe that these differences are good for the movement. They feed it with different energies ... Problems, however, occur when 'Globalize Resistance' becomes 'Monopolize Resistance'; or when the balance between the two orientations becomes disturbed ... Bureaucratization of the movement and the establishing of a forum bureaucracy is more and more obvious ... The danger of turning 'globalization from below' into 'globalization from the middle' is becoming more clearly evident ... It is not that the Forum has been hijacked, but that the anti-authoritarian spirit that has inspired it has been abused. The very slogan 'another world is possible' comes from the Zapatistas.[14]

MR criticized the 'amorphous presentation of "Another Possible World" by the WSF' and offered to 'concretely define an alternative socio-economic structure, as one built on a basis of self-reliance, with a total break from all controls, domination and subjugation by imperialism and the institutions of the world capitalist system'.

As important to the movement as its anti-corporate and anti-imperialist analyses are its hallmarks of inclusivity and direct participation. Violators of these principles are quickly named reformist, not out of a misapprehension of their ideology, but in recognition of their departure from the absolute egalitarianism and openness which many in the movement see as its base of both strength and security in the face of neoliberal pressure and cooptation. In this context, then, 'reformism' is charged against any elitism, failure of solidarity, attempt to marginalize, bureaucratization, channelling, repression of autonomy or barriers to direct participation.

Resources

Third World Network: <www.twnside.org.sg>
Focus on the Global South: <www.focusweb.org>
ATTAC: <www.attac.org>
World Social Forum 2004: <www.wsfindia.org>
Mumbai Resistance: <www.mr2004.org>
Vía Campesina: <www.viacampesina.org>
Jubilee South: <www.jubileesouth.org>
Jubilee North: <www.jubileedebtcampaign.org.uk>
Anti-Privatization Forum: <www.apf.org.za>
Oxfam: <www.oxfam.org>

Notes

1 The International Forum on Globalization, although ideologically radical, is elitist and exclusionary. <www.ifg.org>

2 See PGA Hallmarks at <www.agp.org>; Dakar Declaration at <www.africanfutures.net/af/dakar_decl.htm>

3 Frances Moore Lappé, Joseph Collins and Peter Rosset with Luis Esparza, *World Hunger: 10 Myths,* 4th edn (New York: Grove Press, 1998).

4 Bill Marsden, 'Cholera and the Age of the Water Barons', 3 February 2003, at Center for Public Integrity, the Water Barons Page <www.icij.org/water>

5 See Third World Network <www.twnside.org.sg>

6 See Patrick Bond, *Elite Transitions: Globalisation and the Rise of Economic Fundamentalism* (London: Pluto Press, 2000), or *Talk Left, Walk Right: South Africa's Frustrated Global Reforms* (Natal: University of Natal Press, 2004).

7 United Nations, 'Report on World Conference Against Racism, Racial Discrimination, Xenophobia and Related Intolerance', Durban, August–September 2001, at <www.unhchr.ch/html/racism>

8 Human Rights Watch, 'An Approach to Reparations' (no date), <www.hrw.org/campaigns/race/reparations.htm>

9 Bernard Cassen, 'Inventing ATTAC' (January 2003), pp. 152–74 in Tom Mertes (ed.), *A Movement of Movements: Is Another World Really Possible?* (London: Verso, 2004).

10 Oxfam, 'Intellectual Property and the Knowledge Gap', December 2001 at <www.oxfam.org>

11 Although critical of the USA and EU, 'Rigged Rules and Double Standards' (at <www.maketradefair.com>) was considered unacceptable by the movement because it did not oppose free trade wholesale.

12 William Fisher and Thomas Ponniah (eds), *Another World is Possible: Popular Alternatives to Globalization at the World Social Forum* (London: Zed Books, 2003), p. 6.

13 Ezequiel Adamovsky in openDemocracy, 'What is the Point of Porto Alegre? Activists from Two Generations in Dialogue', 21 January 2003 at <www.opendemocracy.net>

14 Andrej Grubacic, 'Life After Social Forums: New Radicalism and the Questions of Attitude Towards Social Forums', February 2003. Also see Linden Farrer, 'World Forum Movement: Abandon or Contaminate', December 2002. Both at <www.agp.org>

16 | Village life: the subsistence perspective

Urban workers are not the most important constituency of the anti-globalization movement, nor do their interests define it. The defining struggles of the anti-globalization movement are the intense struggles of villagers to maintain control over their lives and protect ecologies against oil exploitation, dams, large landholders (and their paramilitaries), ag-pharma-biotech companies, commercial fishing, aquaculture[1] and forest pre-serves.[2]

Peasants, indigenous fisherfolk and forest gatherers are not seeking to upgrade their status to sweatshop workers, but to protect and develop village life. This means asserting cultural and political autonomy, decommodifying the ecological commons, defending local markets, strengthening traditional livelihoods and organizing endogenous solutions to local problems.

Sadly, urban activists and scholars exhibit consistent rural-phobia, complete with clichéd slurs. Any valorization of village life is portrayed as an impossible move 'back' in history.

As the farmers' organization Vía Campesina makes clear, small-scale farmers in the Global North and Global South alike neither need nor benefit from the kind of progress being offered by Free Trade regimes. To them, 'globalization' means low-quality food 'dumped' into their local markets at prices so heavily subsidized that they are below the cost of production anywhere. This unfair competition drives farmers out of their own local markets. As middlemen become price-setters, even productive and efficient farmers are driven out of their local markets and out of business.

Not only farmers but also artisans such as weavers and soap-makers find their markets undermined by corporate marketing and the globalization of their local markets. Much-celebrated

16 Tojolobal indigenous women and children sit near their homes in a Zapatista village that recuperated these lands in 1995, once run by a large ranch owner (photo by Tim Russo)

microcredit schemes (rescuing the poor by indebting them) are now stumbling.[3] Neoliberal policies allow foreign corporations to invade domestic markets for basic artisanal products such as soap, driving out of business the very micro-enterprises that anti-poverty credit programmes purport to support.[4] Rather than gaining access to 'global markets', small-scale producers want the integrity of their local ones restored.

Even the physical spaces of local markets are under attack, making it obvious that small-scale producers are engaged in class war. As informal economies grow due to shrinking formal employment, repression also grows and vendors organize to defend themselves in many cities. In the Zocalo of Mexico City and the downtown section of San Cristóbal de las Casas, vendors have organized into informal networks to defend themselves from attacks by riot police who routinely break up markets. Vendors have become politicized in Durban, Lima and São Paulo.

Local markets are being redeveloped for trading locally-produced goods in the Global North as well. Local markets foster empathetic knowledge, reintegrating social values into economic choices. The markets also engage entrepreneurs in the collective management of the market (a commons regime). Finally, they facilitate bartering and non-monetary exchanges. These Polanyian[5] developments seem to be of little interest to the socialist left (which often treats small businesses as proto-corporations).

Inspired by these movements, a sector of Global North movements have urged the adoption of a villager orientation in their own societies. Aware of the neocolonial relationship between postmodern consumption and Third World immiseration, activists challenge the conflation of quality of life with standard of living and argue that smaller-scale Northern economies could be more secure and pleasurable as well as more responsible to the Global South. In *The Subsistence Perspective*, Maria Mies and Veronika Bennholdt-Thomsen argue – against most feminists and other modernist authorities of liberation – that subsistence lifestyles are more secure, independent and self-determining than modern ones. They point out that

What is deglobalization?

We are not talking about withdrawing from the international economy. We are speaking about reorienting our economies from the emphasis on production for export to production for the local market; about drawing most of our financial resources for development from within rather than becoming dependent on foreign investment and foreign financial markets; about carrying out the long-postponed measures of income redistribution and land redistribution to create a vibrant internal market that would be the anchor of the economy; about de-emphasizing growth and maximizing equity in order to radically reduce environmental disequilibrium; about not leaving strategic economic decisions to the market but making them subject to democratic choice; about subjecting the private sector and the state to constant monitoring by civil society; about creating a new production and exchange complex that includes community cooperatives, private enterprises, and state enterprises, and excludes TNCs; about enshrining the principle of subsidiarity in economic life by encouraging production of goods to take place at the community and national level if it can be done so at reasonable cost in order to preserve community.

Source: Walden Bello and Nicola Bullard, 'The Global Conjuncture: Characteristics and Challenges', National Convention Against Globalization, New Delhi, 21–23 March 2001

what usually counts as 'liberation' in the North is dependent on the continued impoverization of a South seduced into the treadmill of 'catch-up development' through the 'dead end' industrial system.[6]

Helena Norberg-Hodge, another scholar activist and

advocate of localism, argues that 'communism and capitalism are both centralized, colonial, ruthless. Both exerted pressure on people to stop producing a range of products for local consumption and instead to monocrop for export.' Colin Hines and Tim Lang propose a policy of self-provisioning and international solidarity whose theme is 'protect the local, globally'. Walden Bello articulates a similar project he calls 'deglobalization'.

Critics of localism argue that self-reliance is absurd for the Global South, because manufacturing complex products would be inefficient in a small market and many inputs would have to be purchased.[7] But Global South activists, asserting the viability and benefit of self-reliance, have never demanded a divorce from international trading partners. What they have consistently proposed is self-reliance in food and other basics which can be readily produced locally, providing cultural continuity and full employment.[8] In addition to protection of local and national markets in basic goods, activists argue for protected development of domestic or regional industries, particularly in vital areas (such as pharmaceuticals) in order to increase security and independence. Self-reliant trade strategies are about supporting and protecting local production where it exists and developing it where feasible.

There is a commons

Villagers who defend their livelihoods and the ecologies on which they depend find themselves up against not only a market that recognizes only private property but also erstwhile allies overly impressed by Garrett Hardin's individualistic 'tragedy of the commons'.[9] In fact, commons are only tragically overused when longstanding management regimes are disrupted. The lure of commodification in a context of displacement, impoverization, insecurity and debt constantly endangers commons regimes and must be taken into account in assessing their viability. Forests, water, biodiversity and indigenous science are some of the arenas in which the commons is most actively defended in response to privatization.

In the Global North, activists seeking to restore the commons must struggle not only against its privatization and marketization, but also against psychological colonization. Social movements scholar James Scott notes that what capitalism most wanted people to forget was their right to 'an abundant, self-yielding nature'.[10]

Urban villages

Consistent with the subsistence perspective, permaculture activists and development scholars have developed proposals for transforming unsustainable and alienating cities into networks of low-throughput urban villages. Urban life could be pleasantly and sustainably transformed by working closer to home, walking and biking, retro-fitting urban structures for energy and waste efficiency, depending on edible and functional landscaping, neighbourhood artisanal production, community currencies and barter, and solidarity with nearby rural producers through weekly markets and box schemes.

Romantic social backwardness?

Peasants, fisherfolk, women and indigenous people assert 'farmers' rights', 'food sovereignty', 'multifunctional agriculture', 'reclaim the commons', 'autonomous development',[11] and confidence in their ability to be self-determining.[12] 'Development' as it is used by these movements is defined as an increase in self-determination, autonomy and the ability to solve one's own problems, not as technology and freedom from hard work. A few scholars provide sheafs of philosophy, scientific analysis and social data supporting the viability of local provisioning and autonomy (see resources). Despite the clarity and consistency with which villagers articulate these ideas, the subsistence/village/livelihood perspective has been criticized for not fitting into orthodox liberation theories (or perhaps for what it suggests about the lives of their fashionable authors). This perspective is accused of being simplistic, romantic and hopeless.

Critics focus on presumed reactionary social tendencies

associated with village life such as essentialism, racism or homophobia. Autonomy, traditionalism and even the concept of 'community' frighten the Northern intelligentsia which depends on anonymous urban life for its sense of freedom.

Interestingly, traditional indigenous people claim that their societies allow for much *more complex* individualism than modern or postmodern Western identity. Gender definitions are more fluid and many forms of sexuality and marriage are condoned.[13] Women are not as universally subordinated as they are in the Western imagination.[14] Vandana Shiva argues that village communities provide an 'integrating context' of plurality, not dualism.[15] Studies of recent cases of 'ethnic strife' are revealing 'ancient tribal conflict' to be a convenient myth to cover the elitism which arises when the political economy is disrupted – often by outside forces.[16] But even more basic to the debates is the fact that village-based autonomous movements are often explicitly committed to social diversity, seeing it, along with biological diversity, as the basis of security, wisdom, democracy and pleasure. What is uncomfortable for modern humanitarians is that social justice is not to be sought through the centralized policies of state enforcement but through local autonomy. As indigenous people have consistently asserted, diversity and multiculturalism, if they are indeed to assist 'all cultures to survive and thrive',[17] must ensure autonomous control over resources and institutions.

Many of the difficult problems of modern social theory are addressed handily by today's village activists. The Zapatistas and others are moving along swiftly in addressing women's rights. They and other groups have centred indigenous knowledge in their deliberations and methods, as well as taking direct action against globalization.

Resources

Maria Mies and Veronika Bennholdt-Thomsen, *The Subsistence Perspective: Beyond the Globalized Economy* (London: Zed Books, 2000).

Veronika Bennholdt-Thomsen et al. (eds), *There is an Alternative:*

Subsistence and Worldwide Resistance to Corporate Globalization (London: Zed Books, 2001).

Walden Bello, *Deglobalization: Ideas for a New World Economy* (London: Zed Books, 2003).

Tim Lang and Colin Hines, *The New Protectionism: Protecting the Future Against Free Trade* (New York: New Press, 1993).

Colin Hines, *Localization: A Global Manifesto* (London: Earthscan, 2000).

Gustavo Esteva and Madhu Suri Prakash, *Grassroots Post-Modernism: Remaking the Soil of Cultures* (London: Zed Books, 1998).

The commons: Vandana Shiva et al., *The Enclosure and Recovery of the Commons: Biodiversity, Indigenous Knowledge and Intellectual Property Rights* (New Delhi: Research Foundation for Science, Technology and Ecology, 1997).

The Ecologist, *Whose Common Future?: Reclaiming the Commons* (Philadelphia, PA: New Society, 1993).

Methods for Global South: Stan Burkey, *People First: A Guide to Self-Reliant Participatory Rural Development* (London: Zed Books, 1993).

Martin Khor and Lim Li Lin (eds), *Good Practices and Innovative Experiences in the South* (London: Zed Books, 2002).

WIDE (Web of Information for Development, Special Unit for Technical Cooperation among Developing Countries, United Nations Development Programme), *Sharing Innovative Experiences*. Volumes on: Science and Technology, Small Island Developing States, Livelihood Initiatives, Indigenous and Traditional Practices, Agriculture and Rural Development, Social Organizations and Practices, Indigenous Medicinal Plants, Renewable Energy Sources. At <www.tcdc.undp.org/tcdcweb/experiences>

The Human Right to Livelihood and Land in international law: see <www.pdhre.org/rights/land.html>

Methods for Global North: F. E. Trainer, *The Conserver Society: Alternatives for Sustainability* (London: Zed Books, 1995), online at <www.arts.unsw.edu.au/tsw>

Richard Douthwaite, *Short Circuit: Strengthening Local Economies for Security in an Unstable World* (Chelsea Green Publishing Company, 1998).

Wolfgang Sachs et al., *Greening the North* (London: Zed Books, 2000).

Community currencies: <www.transaction.net>

Urban markets: <www.openair.org>

Permaculture: <www.permaculture.org.uk>

Global directory: <www.permacultureinternational.org>

Notes

1 Commercial fishing and aquaculture also drive down prices through oversupply. See Mangrove Action Project at <www. earthisland.org/map/aqclt.htm> Shrimp farming is affecting coastal communities in Africa, Thailand, India, Bangladesh and Latin America.

2 Global North environmentalism in the Global South puts up fences dividing people from the ecologies on which they have depended with sustainable livelihoods for centuries. Anti-human 'ecological preserves' are a classic example of racist environmentalism. Studies consistently show that the total value of ongoing small-scale sustainable forest extraction is higher than either the timber value or the value of conversion to agricultural use. See Camille Bann, 'Logs or Local Livelihood? The Case for Legalizing Community Control of Forest Lands in Ratanakiri, Cambodia', International Development Research Center, Ottawa, Canada, November 1997; Lucy Emerton, 'Valuing Forest Resources for Conservation Services', Forestry Environmental Accounting Services, African Wildlife Services, n.d.

3 Most famously pioneered by the Grameen Bank (<www. grameen-info.org>), these programmes have been embraced by the World Bank and other traditional lenders. They are criticized as further indebting the poor while avoiding land reform and other needed reforms. More fundamentally, microcredit assumes that poverty can be 'solved' through market participation, without acknowledging that it is built into capitalism and systematically exacerbated by neoliberalism.

4 Thomas Isaac, Michelle Williams, Pinaki Chakraborthy and Binitha V. Thampi, 'Women Neighbourhood Groups: Towards a New Perspective', presented at 'Decentralisation, Sustainable Development and Social Security', St Michael's College, Chertala, India, 11 May 2002 <www.infochangeindia.org>

5 Karl Polanyi argued that social struggle should seek to 're-embed' the market into social values and priorities (*The Great Transformation* [Boston, MA: Beacon Press, 1944]).

6 Maria Mies and Veronika Bennholdt-Thomsen, *The Subsistence Perspective: Beyond the Globalized Economy* (London: Zed Books, 2000). Also see Richard Douthwaite, *The Growth Illusion* (Tulsa, OK: Council Oak, 1993); F. E. Trainer, 'Reconstructing Radical Development Theory', *Alternatives*, 14, 4 (October 1989), pp. 481–515.

7 George Monbiot, 'The Myth of Localism', *Guardian*, 9 September 2003.

8 The 1950s–1960s strategy of 'import substitution' was aggressively delegitimized as it reduced First World export access to Third World markets.

9 Garrett Hardin, 'The Tragedy of the Commons', *Science*, 162 (1968), pp. 1243–8.

10 James C. Scott, *Domination and the Arts of Resistance: Hidden Transcripts* (New Haven, CT: Yale University Press, 1990), p. 81.

11 Dakar Manifesto: Africa: From Resistance to Alternatives, 14 December 2000 <www.50years.org/update/dakar1.html>

12 Vía Campesina founded 1993 (conceptualized 'food sovereignty', presented 'farmers' rights' to UN–FAO in 1996). On Multifunctional Agriculture see Brad DeVries, 'Multifunctional Agriculture in International Context: A Review', October 2000. The Land Stewardship Project at <www.landstewardshipproject. org/mba/MFAReview.pdf> World Forum on Food Sovereignty, Indigenous Peoples' Seattle Declaration, September 2001, Havana, Cuba, November 1999. Third UN of the Peoples, Perugia, Italy, September 1999. Diverse Women for Diversity, Statement to the Plenary of the Fourth Conference of the Parties to the Convention on Biological Diversity, 4 May 1998.

13 Walter L. Williams, *The Spirit and the Flesh: Sexual Diversity in American Indian Culture* (Boston, MA: Beacon Press, 1986).

14 M. Annette Jaimes with Theresa Halsey, *American Indian Women: At the Center of Indigenous Resistance in Contemporary North America* (Boston, MA: South End Press, 1992). Paula Gunn Allen, *The Sacred Hoop: Recovering the Feminine in American Indian Traditions* (Boston, MA: Beacon Press, 1986). Eleanor Burke Leacock, 'Introduction', pp. 7–67 in Frederick Engels, *The Origin of the Family, Private Property and the State* (New York: International Publishers, 1942 [1972]), esp. pp. 29–46. Eleanor Burke Leacock, *Myths of Male Dominance: Collected Articles on Women Cross-Culturally* (New York: Monthly Review Press, 1981).

15 Vandana Shiva, *The Violence of the Green Revolution: Third World Agriculture, Ecology and Politics* (London: Zed Books, 1991), pp. 189–90. Also see Daniel Kemmis, *Community and the Politics of Place* (Norman, OK: University of Oklahoma Press, 1990).

16 Ashis Nandy, *Experiencing Ethnic Violence*, Lecture at UC

Santa Barbara, 7 May 1997. Craig Calhoun, *Nationalism* (Minneapolis: University of Minnesota Press, 1997).

17 Mel King, *Chain of Change: Struggles for Black Community Development* (Boston, MA: South End Press, 1981).

FOUR | Tactics

We are going to take direct action

Participants in the revolt against globalization increasingly conclude that elites cannot be trusted and that institutionalized politics aimed at state power have failed to break free of the neoliberal agenda. It is necessary, then, to imagine and create new political spaces and new forms of power. This creative mandate extends into the methods of struggle itself. As the authors of *We are Everywhere* put it, 'reinventing tactics of resistance has become a central preoccupation'.[1]

A unifying theme among these re/inventions is an emphasis on direct action, occupations, blockades, well-placed carnivals, savvy 'cultural ruptures', and fully-functional alternatives – always surrounded by proper institutional petitions, calm demonstrations, painstaking educational events and astute art.

The most widely recognized and celebrated manifestations of the movement are direct. Worried that protective legislation will be too late, 'midnight gardeners' protect biodiversity by uprooting biotech crops. Certain that 'objections' will be 'brushed aside', forest warriors block the destruction of the forest with their own lives by taking up residence in trees and tunnels in the paths of profit and its 'mindless' roads.[2]

Such direct action raises the costs of corporate operations by disrupting them, exposes the state in its cooperation with them (and its repression of dissent), produces highly symbolic imagery of the issues at stake, and loudly communicates the possibility of effective resistance.

When vegetable gardens are built in such a way that the state surrounds them with hundreds of police with M16s, the issues are well clarified even if the garden does not survive the day. As Starhawk puts it, direct action 'gets in the way of the operations of oppression and poses confrontational alternatives'.[3]

The most ordinary, daily manifestations of the movement are equally direct: street vendors physically defend their space, city people start growing their own food, neighbours organize themselves to fix a local problem. Voltairine de Cleyre, one of the first theorists of direct action, argued: 'Every person who ever had a plan to do anything, and went and did it, or who laid his plan before others, and won their co-operation to do it with him, without going to external authorities to please do the thing for them, was a direct actionist.'[4]

Gandhi's 1908 manifesto for the non-violent liberation of India from colonial rule was entitled *Hind Swaraj*. The struggle for national sovereignty was for him inseparable from the struggle for personal and community 'home rule' – direct action in every aspect of life in lieu of the seductions, professions and rationalizations of 'modern civilization'.

Perhaps articulating a postmodern Gandhism, Reclaim the Streets explains: 'direct action is founded on the idea that people can develop the ability for self-rule only through practice, and proposes that all persons directly decide the important issues facing them'.[5]

Resources

Historical and cultural analysis: Tim Jordan, *Activism!: Direct Action, Hacktivism, and the Future of Society.* 2002: Reaktion Books, London.

Practical instruction: Starhawk, *Webs of Power.* 2002: New Society Publishers. or www.starhawk.org

Notes

1 Notes from Nowhere (ed.), *We are Everywhere* (London: Verso, 2003) p. 174.

2 Ali Begbie, 'Pollok Free Statement', in Stacy Wakefield and Grrrt, *Not for Rent: Conversations with Creative Activists in the UK* (New York: Evil Twin Publications, 1995, 2003).

3 Starhawk, 'Québec City: Beyond Violence and Nonviolence' April 2001 at <www.starhawk.org>

4 Voltairine de Cleyre (1866–1912), 'Direct Action'. Available at <praxeology.net/VC-DA.htm>

5 <www.reclaimthestreets.net>

17 Acampamento Nova Encruzilhada Natalino,
Rio Grande do Sul (photo Arquivo MST,
Movimento dos Trabalhadores Rurais Sem
Terra, Brasil)

17 | Criminal reconnections: decommodification

Anti-globalization is far from limited to protest and opposition. Its most confrontational moments are less ephemeral and rhetorical – they are the refusals to leave land slated for 'development', the autonomous zones established and defended by the (formerly) poor and voiceless, and the defence of rights to 'goods and services' (basic elements of life such as seeds and water, recently commodified).

One of the most powerful forms of direct action aims immediately to decommodify basic needs and develop alternative methods of meeting them. Such projects facilitate the development of autonomy. One way of describing these practices is DIY (do-it-yourself).

Reconnections

The struggles against the privatization of telephones, transportation and other basic services include direct action 'reconnections' of utilities and removals of pre-paid electricity and water meters. These tactics are particularly strong in South Africa, as militant grassroots group engage increasingly violent police forces in their efforts to prevent or reverse evictions and cut-offs.[1] The African National Congress describes as 'criminals' community technicians who reconnect households despite the fact that the post-apartheid constitution guaranteed rights to basic services. Energetic youth around the world share technology for outwitting subways, cable TV servers, telephone systems and the commodification of entertainment.

Pirate radio

As media monopolies have become more pervasive, the alternative press struggles to maintain its audience, operating funds and independence. Undercutting public funding of community broadcasting has been a standard element of structural adjustment in North and South alike. While print media are hard to control and exclude, television and radio are easily privatized by the manipulation of the licensing requirements. Pirate radio stations with tiny, economical broadcasting ranges evolved as a form of alternative media, but since they are now often illegal and increasingly criminalized, they are unavoidably activist. To prevent capture of equipment and media activists pirate radio stations are sometimes mobile.

Copwatch

Disheartened by complaint procedures, toothless oversight committees and systematic human rights violations, observers take direct action to intimidate the police into behaving legally. Armed with recording devices, knowledge of the law and official markings, watchers patrol neighbourhoods and political or social events expected to receive discriminatory policing, observing police violations of the law. Occasionally copwatch teams make an effort to annoy or distract the police with some legal debate in such a way that the detainees are able to escape. More often their presence tones down police behaviour. When this fails, their evidence is useful in court and in police accountability campaigns.

Food Not Bombs

Begun in 1980, Food Not Bombs is a decentralized network of local chapters in Europe, the Americas and Australia. Chapters glean vegetarian food from early points in the waste stream and feed people as often as possible. This action aims to expose the connections between war and poverty and between industrial agriculture and violence to workers, animals, the earth and health. FNB action also challenges the commodification of food, waste and hunger. Many chapters provide food at political gatherings as well, as one of many forms of self-provisioning. Food Not Bombs makes decisions inclusively, and has no leaders.

The name Food Not Bombs states our most fundamental principle: That our society needs things that give life not things that give death ... At demonstrations and our daily servings we concentrate on serving food in a peaceful and respectful manner, thereby creating a safe environment for people to eat in ... The food we serve also expresses our commitment to non-violence.[2]

Occupy, resist, produce

Housing squats are widespread in the Global South. The most sophisticated is the MST in Brasil, which organizes whole communities to invade unused land, maintain an occupation, build a settlement, and commence production. After establishing the community, the MST goes to work in the courts, demanding that the community be given legal status. The MST has already expanded to Bolivia and is working with movements in many parts of the world.

On the outskirts of Cairo, thousands have attempted to build their own future in the squatted City of the Dead, built among and sometimes even inside the tombs there. The community includes autonomous schools and other institutions.[3] Similar illegally squatted communities form rings of poverty and protest around many South African cities; they are routinely subject to brutal evictions, though people repeatedly defend and retake their homes. The same network of activists who take direct action against privatization also organize militant action blocking evictions or returning people to their homes.

Major squatting communities are active and organized throughout Asia. In Japan, groups occupy parks and subways, using tactics such as the 'barrack concept' which refers to easily assembled and disassembled buildings designed to be erected on public lands.[4] In Hong Kong, the half-century-old autonomous community of Diamond Hill resists ongoing gentrification and evictions.[5] In Seoul, South Korea, a grassroots organization by the name of Seochulhyup (Council of the Evicted) physically defends squats and street vendors from police evictions in over fifty districts.[6]

In Europe and North America, squats are primarily focused on providing free housing for those who need it by occupying unused buildings. As in the rest of the world, squatted spaces are subject to arbitrary and violent police action and evictions, often simply resulting in clearing the building to sit empty and unused – the sad fate also of many community gardens.

'Occupy, resist, produce' is also the concept used by Argentinian workers who expropriate closed factories and begin production as 'workers without bosses'. Of the hundreds of occupied factories involving more than 10,000 workers, dozens have also won legal expropriation status from the government. Venezuelan workers have also been occupying factories, winning their first legal expropriation in January, 2005. Under President Chávez's plan for 'endogenous development', any companies who close and abandon their workforce will have their factories seized, nationalized and put under joint worker–state control.[7]

Social centres

Strongest in Italy, replicated erratically across Europe and Latin America and attempted occasionally in North America, squatted social centres directly challenge private property, the commodification and control of education, music and art, and the criminalization of youth. The social centres provide accessible space for art production and exhibitions, musical events (minimal fees help to pay activists' legal costs), movies and performance theatres, participatory education, yoga and dance classes, community conferences, infoshops, workshops, bars, graffiti, gyms, skateboard ramps, alternative media and communal childcare. Sometimes the people who live in the social centre protect it.[8] Social centres thrive in the intersection of marginalized artists, underground music and activist communities.

Infoshops

Physical spaces are precious for activist communities, but hard to sustain financially. One of the more sustainable sort of community spaces, which makes good use of very small rooms, is the infoshop. These are libraries built, maintained and run by activist communities to provide free or low-cost access to hard-to-find political books, how-to guides for things like gardening and women's health, international activist news, local and national independent distribution items such as zines, political art and conversation, activist archives, reading and discussion groups, announcement boards for swaps, rides and events, and perhaps a few computers for internet access and leaflet production. While a permanent space is desirable, infoshops can be temporary, event-specific or mobile.

Guerrilla gardening

Increasingly across the Global South, urban agriculture is an important part of food security.[9] Gardens may be formalized with legal status to provide long-term neighbourhood food supplies, they may be marginal transgressions of public or private property aiming quietly to transform the landscape, or they may take the form of major invasions of lawns, highways or junctions.

In all of these forms, they simultaneously provide a number of different functions, in addition to free food. They reveal the brutality of the privatized food system. They draw attention to and dare to transform the idiocy and elitism of inedible land-scaping. They beautify barren urban spaces and/or challenge the beauty standards of non-productive landscaping styles. They often model sustainable water and waste systems. They model taking direct action on local needs (hunger, open spaces and recreation). They valorize farms, farmers and farming. They are intergenerational and multicultural spaces of education, celebration and relaxation. They rupture the mechanisms and culture of commodification. They expose the policies of violence and exclusion which govern public space. 'Under the cover of darkness, we plant seeds and seedlings in all those neglected corners of public space. Join us as we vandalise the city with nature.'[10]

Resources

Reconnections: Anti-Privatization Forum, South Africa: <www.apf. org.za>

Pirate radio: Ron Sakolsky and Stephen Dunifer (eds), *Seizing the Airwaves: A Free Radio Handbook* (AK Press) online at <www. infoshop.org/texts/seizing/toc.html>

Radio 4 All has links all over the world: <www.radio4all.org>

Copwatch: online video at: <www.guerrillanews.com/copwatch>

Berkeley Copwatch: <www.berkeleycopwatch.org> Video *These Streets are Watching*, $20 to Copwatch, 2022 Blake Street, Berkeley, CA 94704

Food Not Bombs: C. T. Butler and Keith McHenry, *Food Not Bombs: How to Feed the Hungry and Build Community,* 20th anniversary edn (Tucson, AZ: Sharp Press, 2000). <www.foodnotbombs.net>

Squats: Antonio Azuela, Emilio Duhau and Enrique Ortiz, *Evictions and the Right to Housing: Experience from Canada, Chile, the Dominican Republic, South Africa, and South Korea* (Ottawa: International Development Resource Center, 1998), book online at <www.web.idrc.ca/en/ev-32000-201-1-DO_TOPIC.html>

Asian Coalition for Housing Rights: <www.achr.net>

Society for the Promotion of Area Resource Centers, India: <www. sparcindia.org>

Housing and social centres squatted: <www.squat.net>

Social centres: Stacy Wakefield and Grrrt, *Not for Rent: Conversations with Creative Activists in the U.K.* (New York: Evil Twin Publications, 1995, 2003).

World Social Centers.org at <www.ecocon.org/socialcenters>

De Vrije Ruimte (The Free Space): <www.vrijeruimte.nl.> They conducted a survey of free places and published a brochure 'Laat 1000 vrijplaatsen bloeien' (Let 1000 free places bloom) <www.vrijeruimte.nl/1000bloeien>

Radical Routes, UK: <www.radicalroutes.org.uk>

Infoshops around the world: <www.infoshop.org>

Urban gardens: Maria Caridad Cruz and Roberto Sánchez Medina, *Agriculture in the City: A Key to Sustainability in Havana, Cuba* (International Development Research Center, Ian Randle Publishers, 2003).

Resource Center on Urban Agriculture and Forestry: <www.ruaf. org>

Urban Agriculture Notes worldwide documentation: <www. cityfarmer.org>

Expropriated factories: Workers without Bosses solidarity network for Argentina's occupied factories: <www.workers withoutbosses.net>

Notes

1 Patrick Bond, 'Power to the People in South Africa: Operation Khanyisa! and the Fight Against Electricity Privatization', *Multinational Monitor*, 23, 1/2 (January–February 2002). See the Anti-Privatization Forum at <www.apf.org.za>, the Soweto Electricity Crisis Committee and Operation Khanyisa. Also see Chris Smith, 'Guerrilla Technicians Challenge the Privatization of South Africa's Public Resources', *In These Times* (30 August 2002).

2 Food Not Bombs, 'Statement of Non-Violence'.

3 Jeffrey A. Nedoroscik, *City of the Dead: A History of Cairo's Cemetery Communities* (Westport, CT: Greenwood, 1997).

4 Nojiren and Inoken: <www.jca.apc.org/nojukusha/nojiren>

5 Wanda Baxter, 'Squatters in Hong Kong: Revisiting Squatting Settlements in a Booming Economy', Research and Scholarship Archives, 26 June 2000 <www.ucalgary.ca/unicomm/Research/smart.htm>

6 Text adapted from Jason Adams and Amory Starr, 'Anti-Globalization: The Global Fight for Local Autonomy', *New Political Science*, 25, 1 (March 2003). See Antonio Azuela, Emilio Duhan and Enrique Ortiz, *Evictions and the Right to Housing: Experience from Canada, Chile, the Dominican Republic, South Africa, and South Korea* (Ottawa: International Development Resource Center, 1998).

7 Jonah Gindin, 'Venezuela's Venepal Under Workers Control After Bankruptcy and Expropriation', 20 January 2005, <www.venezuelanalysis.com>

8 Adam Bregman, 'Italy's Cultural Underground', *Alternative Press Review*, 6, 1 (Spring 2001).

9 Jac Smit, Annu Ratta and Joe Nasr, *Urban Agriculture: Food, Jobs and Sustainable Cities*, Habitat II Series (UNDP, 1996). Jac Smit and Joe Nasr, 'Farming in Cities: Raising Food in Cities Improves Urban Landscapes and Residents' Diets Using Urban-generated Waste', *Context* (quarterly journal of humane sustainable culture), 42: *A Good Harvest* (Autumn 1995): 20; <www.context.org>.

10 Toronto Public Space Committee<publicspace.ca/gardeners.htm>

18 upper: Zapatista support base members halt a military incursion into Galeana in January 1998, just two weeks after paramilitaries massacred forty-eight indigenous men, women, children and elders in Acteal (photo by Tim Russo)   lower: Dissenters lockdown during the 2000 Philadalphia Convention at which George W. Bush was nominated Presidential Candidate (photo by Tim Russo)

18 | The streets belong to the people

Before, during and after the hegemony of representative democracies, political power has been exercised in the streets. With limited or meaningless direct access to the formal political process, most people express their outrage, dissent and immediate needs through embodied collective action in public space. Thus 'riots' were the immediate response to implementation of Structural Adjustment Programmes across the Global South: 'The protesters take to the streets because this is the form of expression available to them. The lack of other venues and social mechanisms is not their creation.'[1]

So long as people solve their problems at their own kitchen tables (or simply become despondent),[2] the streets are quiet. Recognizing that our personal problems are indeed public ones,[3] we may engage in public action, whose initial stages (phone calls, letters, donations) cause little trouble or disruption. When all avenues have been exhausted, we seize public space. And for the poor, other avenues are few and weak. The streets are the final, common power for every sector of society. Indeed, they measure the degree to which people understand their lives and fates as 'public'.

And the power of the streets is no shabby last resort. The March 2005 road blockades in Bolivia cost the country $13.8 million per day. By stopping the flow of goods, workers and police, people can collectively exert tremendous power. Usurping transportation routes makes unavoidable the urgency of grievances against the mundane priorities of commerce.

Since the street is so crucial to commerce and rule, the state asserts military, legal and ideological control over it. Any disruption of commerce, even if resolutely pacifist, meets with an increasingly violent military response. Disruptions are often criminalized and both private property and traffic flow are sanctified in the law, so that their violation brings greater penalties than crimes against persons, such as rape. The ideology of consumerism contributes to smooth traffic flow by convincing people that their good taste, bargain hunting and buying power can solve their problems. If these don't work, voting will.

The right to disrupt 'business as usual' in the interest of political voice is protected in international law, but whether this right will exist on any given day is entirely a matter of numbers. Overwhelming numbers of people in the streets, particularly if they are on indefinite strike and remain steadfast despite repression, is a sure, simple and non-violent way of exerting power. It is also, for reasons which perplex organizers and observers, relatively rare. When there aren't enough numbers simply to overwhelm the authorities – which is most of the time – intricate tactics are organized.

What do you need to shut down the World Bank? Well, between the ten of us, we had: loads of bilingual leaflets (which we very much hoped said what they were meant to), a gas mask and first aid kit each, one press accreditation pass for attending the official meetings, lots of silver-sequinned items of clothing, one laptop computer (for uploading to www.prague.indymedia.org), far too many mobile phones, a large collection of pirate radio broadcast equipment, one thousand hot pink stickers that said 'Lide ne Zisk!' (Czech for 'People not profit'), one thousand red, green, black, and pink balloons that also said – in Czech and English – 'create the world you want to live in', and a very large helium canister ...

We had a stack of cyclists. We had the gorgeous Tactical Frivolity dancers. We had samba instruments, and we (almost, give us a few more practices) knew how to use them. We had some people willing to be part of prisoner support, and some ready to take on co-ordinating communications ... And – as the days passed – increasing amounts of chocolate and small scraps of paper with important things written on them ...

There was never enough time, really. Endless meetings occurred at the convergence centre ... as more and more people speaking half a dozen different languages attempted to reach consensus regarding a blockading plan ... In the gaps, our ... cluster debated its way through the options of how to participate autonomously within the plan ... We had little idea of what would happen, how it would happen, what exactly we wanted to happen, and why we were blockading the delegates in rather than out of the conference (the stated plan) but we were trying to figure all this out as fast and as democratically as possible.[4]

In the Global South, main roads are barricaded, cutting off food and inputs to cities for days or weeks. The barricades are defended to the death, and the government often must acquiesce. Smaller (and generally less fierce) barricades are erected to protect neighbourhoods or street occupations themselves in the Global North. The composition of the barricades and the tactics used for their defence vary with the exact mix of political and physical resources available to police and barricaders.

Other methods of controlling the streets include lockdowns, sitdowns, large props and parties.

Lockdowns are a tactic of blockading in which people use some sort of locking mechanism (bike locks, handcuffs, chains and padlocks) to attach themselves either to each other (so that they are immovably in the only path of what they are opposing) or to doorways, equipment, etc. (to prevent their use). Those immobilized in the lockdown are supported by an equally committed group which shields and cares for them. Lockdowns use the vulnerability of the body to raise the stakes with the police, who can cause severe injury if they are not very careful. They also increase the cost and time for the state to eliminate the manifestation, keeping dissent more visible for a longer period of time. Lockdowns maximize the impact of a few committed persons. The symbolic non-violent imagery of the lockdown is also useful educationally.

Sitdowns require larger numbers of people. People are calm and peaceable, they listen to educational speeches and meanwhile block the way. In addition to the calm occupation of space, sitdowns threaten disciplined incipient riot. Large props such as sandboxes, impromptu living rooms with couches and rugs, inflatable whales, sound stages, stalled trucks and parade

187

Reclaim the Streets

Ultimately it is in the streets that power must be dissolved: for the streets where daily life is endured, suffered and eroded, and where power is confronted and fought, must be turned into the domain where daily life is enjoyed, created and nourished.

The street is an extremely important symbol because your whole enculturation experience is geared around keeping you out of the street ... The idea is to keep everyone indoors. So, when you come to challenge the powers that be, inevitably you find yourself on the curbstone of indifference, wondering 'should I play it safe and stay on the sidewalks, or should I go into the street?' And it is the ones who are taking the most risks that will ultimately effect the change in society ...

We are about taking back public space from the enclosed private arena. At its simplest this is an attack on cars as a principal agent of enclosure. It's about reclaiming the streets as public inclusive space from the private exclusive use of the car. But we believe in this as a broader principle, taking back those things which have been enclosed within capitalist circulation and returning them to collective use as a commons ...

In this sense the streets are the alternative and subversive form of the mass media. Where authentic communication, immediate and reciprocal, takes place.

To 'reclaim the streets' is to act in defence of and for common ground. To tear down the fence of enclosure that profit-making demands. And the Street Party – far from being just anti-car – is an explosion of our suppressed potential, a celebration of our diversity and a chorus of voices in solidarity ...

Carnival celebrates temporary liberation from the prevailing truth and the established order; it marks the suspension of all hierarchical rank, privileges, norms

> and prohibitions. Carnival is not a spectacle seen by the people; they live in it, and everyone participates because its very idea embraces all the people.

floats are useful to expand a human blockade or occupation and hinder removal. Some props incorporate the lockdown tactic of vulnerable bodies, such as unwieldy puppets, stilt-walkers and tripods (which elevate a person high above the roadway). Props, particularly expensive ones and those with vulnerable human parts, require the protection of a surrounding large group of mobile people, whose attention is best held by a good party.

The immediate impact of road occupations on the institutions they seek to disrupt varies widely, and the briefest ones generate negligible leverage. Nevertheless, 'taking the street', even briefly, is effective in a number of other ways. The return to the streets as a location of political activity is a global gesture that communicates its concerns and intentions easily across culture, language and all natural and artificial divides. It communicates the fact that people are dissenting, that they are willing to take risks, and that for some reason they find it necessary to use this most basic voice which, not incidentally, tells the world something about what is going on under the purportedly democratic regimes. The creation of public space in the midst of the street is an abrupt and egalitarian educational event, a rupture which actively transforms conceptions of the political.

Taking the streets is a powerful act, most importantly because it enables strangers to find a sense of community. In the ringing words of an Argentinian named Pablo: 'security used to be in the bank, and insecurity was in the streets. Now insecurity is in the bank ... And security is in the streets, with our neighbors.'[5] This experience of community brings great joy and encourages people in daring to dissent and realize dreams made all the more urgent and precious in the context of

The streets belong to the people

repression. Reclaiming the street is the beginning of reclaiming our societies and our lives.

Popular in the Global North as a form of barricade and occupation are street festivals with music, dancing and a carnival atmosphere. Many of these have been inspired by Reclaim the Streets, a tactic first used in London. RTS' cleverly organized and highly politicized parties represent a profound confrontation with the forces of privatization and criminalization while asserting confidence and wild delight in all things people-centred.

In addition to marches, blockades and political carnivals, the streets are a site of struggle for livelihood, as homeless persons, vendors and youth fight on a daily basis to protect the streets as a commons for self-expression, recreation, informal economy and subsistence. Art and civil disobedience contest privatization and criminalization by making the impoverishment of people and culture visible and by drawing out and exposing the repressive violence of the state.

Resources

Temma Kaplan, *Taking Back the Streets: Women, Youth, and Direct Democracy* (Berkeley: University of California Press, 2003).

Jeff Ferrell, *Tearing Down the Streets: Adventures in Urban Anarchy* (London: Palgrave, 2001).

Reclaim the Streets: <www.reclaimthestreets.net>

Notes

1 Michael Hardt and Antonio Negri, 'What the Protesters in Genoa Want', pp. 101–3 in *On Fire: The Battle of Genoa and the Anti-capitalist Movement* (London: One-off Press, 2001), p. 102.

2 See James Petras, 'Neo-liberalism, Popular Resistance and Mental Health', *Rebelión*, 17 December 2002, at <www.rebelion. org/petras/english>

3 A connection described by C. Wright Mills in 1951 as the exercise of 'sociological imagination'.

4 Penny of Earth First!, 'The Pink-and-Silver Samba Block does Prague!' at <www.nadir.org/nadir/initiativ/agp/s26/praga/pinkrep. htm>

5 PGA Argentina pages at <www.agp.org>

19 | Culture jamming

Michel Foucault's concern that we might lose track of our genuine desires seems prescient now that government policy is developed jointly with professional public relations consultants to be cross-promoted through the multimedia tentacles of consolidated entertainment/news purveyors.

Important ideological projects, conveyed in exceedingly subtle as well as overt ways, capture the implicit premises of global culture: consumption is citizenship, capitalism is democracy, globalization nurtures multiculturalism and family, empire is humanitarian intervention, personal responsibility explains suffering, and individualism is more desirable, interesting and fulfilling than community. Alongside efforts to reclaim farms, services, resources, housing and political space, alterglobalization activists recognize the need to reclaim the complex terrain where psychology and ideology meet – a terrain nearly totally determined by saturation advertising. Warfare in this over-stimulated stream of seductive and purloined images requires technical savvy, sharp wit, rapid response and, increasingly, crampons and 'extreme' athletic skills since the mainstream media refuse even to *sell* space to critics.[1]

The resulting cultural jujitsu has transformed the imagery of activism. Activists now sport aesthetically tight, quirkily entertaining, and ferociously clever anti-ads produced by our own artists, writers and techies. Video geeks are painstakingly modifying news and entertainment imagery to show Bush and Blair singing 'Endless Love' to each other[2] or to unveil Tolkien's prophetic analysis of the relationship between liberals and anarchists in *The Lord of the Rings*.[3] Pranksters pose as corporate executives and promote draconian policies to unflinching audiences.[4] The movement has achieved new heights of satire.

This is culture jamming. It loses nothing of the synthetic appeal of advertising and music videos, but turns their

19 The first photo which hit the internet following the assassination of Carlo Giuliani in Genoa at the July 2001 G8 protests was a culturejam. The blood was changed into the shape of Italy (image from Italy Indymedia)

aesthetic tricks (and even their own images) against them. Brilliant imagery and hip analysis are combined with aggressive stuntwork and property violations in the form of banner hangs, billboard modifications, newspaper inserts, pranks, flash mobs and logo sabotage. Culture jamming is more than this, though. It is at once a deeply reflexive method of psychic healing (see *AdBusters* magazine), a community of artists (see Loesje), and institutions (see the MoveOn 'Bush in 30 seconds' ad contest).

Websites for some culture jamming groups even mimic corporate sales. The Billboard Liberation Front offers 'a broad range of black-bag operations and cultural jam services, from project management and subversion consulting to media manipulation and thought placement'. RTMark organizes 'mutual funds' to 'improve culture'. Perhaps unlike other tactics, as culture jamming catches on it becomes *more* decentralized and grassroots. Low-tech interventions continue as activists use chalk, graffiti and stickers to intervene in the cultural landscape. *AdBusters* is now the old guard.

> Then there was the Loesje statement of 'WAR – Do Not Feed' analogue to the signs found in zoos on the cages of dangerous animals. Loesje is something special here in the Netherlands. It has been around for 15 years now and what they do, and nobody really knows who THEY are, is make one-liner posters and stick them to walls in public places. These one-liners are most of the time heavily reflective on political and cultural events. For 15 years now they have manage[d] to stay away from aligning themselves to any particular political party and are truly independent and open-minded.[5]

Today's slick culture jamming may have a striking new aesthetic, but has its roots in the political art of dada (1917–), surrealism (1924–) and situationism (1957–) as well as in folk traditions of graffiti and street theatre which use materials at hand to interrupt the flow of hegemonic culture. These traditions convey complex theories of cynicism, the proper relations between art and politics, and the transformative power

Culture jamming

of self-creation. The situationists recognized the dangers of appropriation and the rapid reassembly of critical voices that we see today. Their concept of 'recuperation' referred to what they understood to be the fatal commodification of revolutionary ideas. The situationists increasingly renounced any kind of art which could be commodified.

AdBusters promptly commodified itself, selling the magazine at supermarkets, holiday gift sets of adbust postcards, and their own sneakers designed to 'reclaim culture' and 'reassert consumer sovereignty over capitalism' through a 'worldwide consumer cooperative'.

Resources

Tim Jordan, *Activism!: Direct Action, Hacktivism, and the Future of Society* (London: Reaktion Books, 2002).

Els van der Plas (ed.), *Creating Culture in Defiance: Spaces of Freedom* (The Hague: Prince Claus Fund, 2002); <www.prince clausfund.nl>

The Biotic Baking Brigade, *Pie Any Means Necessary* (Oakland, CA: AK Press, 2004), or <bioticbakingbrigade.org>

AdBusters online: <www.adbusters.org> *Adbusters: Journal of the Mental Environment*, 1243 West 7th Avenue, Vancouver, BC, V6H 1B7 Canada.

Loesje International: <www.loesje.org>

Graffiti (lots of links): <www.artcrimes.org>

Culture Jam Idea Bank and Mutual Funds: <www.RTMark.com>

Pranks: <www.theyesmen.org>

Flashmob.com

Billboard Liberation Front: <www.billboardliberation.com>

Activist Climbing for Banner Hangs: <ruckus.org/resources/manuals/climbing>

Situationism: Guy Debord, *The Society of the Spectacle* (1967) <www.nothingness.org>

Versionfest Art/Technology Network: <www.versionfest.org>

Notes

1 Coy Barefoot, 'Jumping Over the Dead Left', *AlterNet*, 10 September 2001, at <www.alternet.org>

2 Johan Söderberg, for Kobra (Swedish TV), Read My Lips, at <www.politicalhumor.about.com/library/multimedia/bushblair_ endlesslove.mov>

3 Fellowship of the Ring of Free Trade, at <www.passionbomb.com/video/ringfreetrade.htm>

4 <www.theyesmen.org>

5 Wouter Hijink, 'Report from Amsterdam, "WAR: Do Not Feed!"', *CounterPunch*, 15 February 2003.

20 Media activists from Mexico, Korea and the United States work together on Radio Hurakan, an internet radio stream, airing twenty-four hours a day during the September 2003 demonstrations against the World Trade Organization in Cancún, Mexico. Radio Hurakan formed one of several collective media projects at the Cancún Indymedia Center, where 300 independent journalists worked together to offer alternative media coverage (photo by Tim Russo)

20 | Be the media: Independent Media Centers

While there is nothing new about the idea that media ought to be independent (of the state, of elites, of each other), several forms of media activism converged quite recently in the creation of a promising new institution, the Independent Media Center. The idea of a global alternative media network had been discussed at the 1996 and 1997 Zapatista Encuentros (in Chiapas and Spain). Of course, there were plenty of activist media collectives and projects to draw on, as well as community access media (radio[1] and TV), activist technology collectives, international listservs,[2] internet-based 'webcasting' and open publishing groups and methods.

In 1996, people working with Community Activist Technology in Australia reported on a community radio conference by avoiding the 'official story of what the conference was about'. Instead they 'tried to break through the hierarchy and have people reporting on the sessions'. This project was the basis of the first automated open-publishing software. When Reclaim the Streets took the City of London in June 1999, their media team set up an operation to upload media live during the carnival. For the Seattle WTO protests in November 1999 (n30), the first IndyMedia Center (IMC) was organized collaboratively to provide shared space in a shopfront at the heart of the actions. This IMC established many of what are now IMC traditions, such as sharing equipment and footage.

Photos, text, audio and video were put on to the website, alongside a newswire with live reports updated by the minute. These could be viewed directly by readers with internet access, and also were downloaded, printed and redistributed or rebroadcast in various localities. 'Floating above the tear gas was a pulsing infosphere of enormous bandwidth, reaching around the planet.'[3] The IMC became an archive for photo,

About Indymedia

The Independent Media Center is a network of collectively run media outlets for the creation of radical, accurate, and passionate tellings of the truth. We work out of a love and inspiration for people who continue to work for a better world, despite corporate media's distortions and unwillingness to cover the efforts to free humanity. <www.indymedia.org>

video and audio materials, enabling the production of videos drawing on footage from more than 100 cameras. It was also a space for spontaneous collaborations by journalists who produced a daily newspaper, a daily thirty-minute TV programme (uplinked daily on donated satellite time), and micro-radio. According to Jeff Perlstein, the structure of the first IMC was greatly influenced by Zapatista principles of the importance of process, reclaiming space, decentralization, and 'one no, many yeses'.[4]

Two years after Seattle, there were sixty IMCs in twenty countries on six continents. Five years after Seattle, there are over 130 IMCs operating in seven languages. About fifty of these are in the USA, which has the most localized network. Nearly forty are in Europe, most being national, but some countries have more than one. Israel, Palestine and Iraq all have IMCs. By several measures, Indymedia is now the largest news network on the planet.

In addition to its global connections, Indymedia is distinct from many other alternative media in emphasizing news over commentary, prioritizing coverage of activism and encouraging direct reporting. Indymedia recognizes alternative media as *part of* social movements[5] – a mission Subcomandante Marcos advanced in 1997, saying that 'the work of independent media is to tell the history of social struggle in the world'.[6] Media activist and analyst Dorothy Kidd describes the new media of which Indymedia is a part as making a qualitative shift from 'alternative media' to decentralized 'autonomous communications' focused less on reporting and analysis and more on 'direct witness' from activists. Indymedia's distinct style of reporting echoes the movement's imagery and strategy of 'one no, many yeses', 'a carnival of representation, a plurality of perspectives, images and modes of address'.[7]

From the beginning, the London-based IMC collective regarded Indymedia as a project in both virtual and physical space. Open publishing allowed the streets to enter cyberspace, but it also brought technology to the streets. From the mission statement: 'Through this system of "Direct Media", Indymedia erodes the dividing line between reporters and reported, between active producers and passive audience: people are enabled to speak for themselves.' Direct media = media as party, education, direct action, entertainment, empowerment. Film screenings, radio programs, printed

---

Aotearoa Independent Media Centre (AIM)

We AIM to provide a decentralised internet media forum for voices and viewpoints currently suppressed or distorted by the commercial imperatives of corporate and government-backed media ... We AIM to create 'virtual' and real-life networks between grass roots community groups and NGOs (Non-Governmental Organisations) ... We AIM to open access to media technology so all groups can speak for themselves ... We AIM to promote the participation of citizens in social, environmental and political issues that affect communities at local, national and global levels ... We take AIM at profit-driven media and its manipulation of the public mind ... We believe that people taking back their voices is both vital to empowering individuals to define themselves as citizens rather than consumers, and creating sustainable communities. <www.indymedia.org.nz>

Be the media

materials and public access terminals created a presence outside the web ... If you have neither money nor the will to acquire it, how do you run a media centre in London, with its long history of capitalism and its attitude of charging £2 for every breath you take? ... Unlimited public-ness can be scary, but as a large network, IMC UK relies even more than before on openness and transparency.[8]

What made possible this qualitative and quantitative leap forward was the proliferation of collaboration precipitated by n30, new technology and a well-established tradition in tech and activist communities of democracy and openness expressed simultaneously in the shape of the technology and in the social organization of use. IMCs have fiercely defended both local autonomy and solidarity, providing an excellent model for the relations between those priorities. 'Self-rule of local sites begins to prefigure autonomous communications centered in the dreams, realities, and communications needs of each locale.'[9]

The Indymedia editorial structure is participatory and democratic, as are all aspects of the network's process and progress.

A working definition of open publishing: Open publishing means that the process of creating news is transparent to the readers. They can contribute a story and see it instantly appear in the pool of stories publicly available. Those stories are filtered as little as possible to help the readers find the stories they want. Readers can see editorial decisions being made by others. They can see how to get involved and help make editorial decisions. If they can think of a better way for the software to help shape editorial decisions, they can copy the software because it is free and change it and start their own site. If they want to redistribute the news, they can, preferably on an open publishing site.[10]

The IMC process does not see itself as neutral but as activist and subject to repression and cooptation. IMC servers have been shut down and confiscated by law enforcement. In 2002 an offered Ford Foundation grant for Indymedia conferences was rejected, with IMC-Argentina expressing particular concern. The collective priorities of the network currently are helping to build IMCs in the Global South, increasing translation and issues of process (such as the procedure for establishing new IMCs). These priorities are visible in the choice of software. The open-source software used by many IMCs is Mir, preferred for its multilingual content and its capacity 'to be run on less than top of the line hardware through extensive static caching'.[11]

Assisting the growth of the IMCs has been the growth of activist technology organizations embracing many of the same principles. National or regional collectives provide web-hosting, email and chat (live discussions), democratizing access to computer media by providing free services to activists and activist organizations, actively avoiding the corporatization of the internet, and also maximizing the security of activist communications.

While the technology seems to have been the most powerful contribution, particularly in reducing the costs of production and distribution, it is important not to overestimate its novel, generative contributions. Indymedia has not always paid attention to its predecessors, particularly when those are in the Global South. As Dorothy Kidd points out, Indymedia has much to learn from methods of 'interactive autonomy'[12] already established, particularly by South–South alternative media networks. This history includes choosing the technology that is most easily available – the task then being to 'liberate the technology to put it in the hands of the women where the action is'.[13] The newly popular notion of 'tactical' media is a practice well-established in the Global South.

> We are the network, all of us who speak and listen. (EZLN, Second Declaration of La Realidad, 1996)[14]

Each IMC local editorial collective mixes local news with global news at will, expressing and promoting solidarity with geographically distant but otherwise proximate struggles.

Resources

Global Indymedia site with links everywhere: <www.indymedia.org>

Reports/blog of an itinerant indymedia activist: <www.anarchogeek.com>

Activist technology collectives: <www.tao.ca>; <nadir.org>, <autistici.org>; <inventati.org>; <sindominio.net ecn>; <nodo50.0g.>; <www.antenna.nl>

FIRE: <www.fire.or.cr>

Organic Chaos Network with good list of links to activist media: <www.antenna.nl/organicchaos>

Thomas Harding, *The Video Activist Handbook* (London: Pluto Press, 2001).

Notes

1 For a particularly clear explanation of the role of women's radio in the Global South and the fundamental contributions of international media networks, see Dorothy Kidd, 'Which Would You Rather: Seattle or Porto Alegre?', *Our Media, Not Theirs*, Barcelona, July 2002, at <www.ourmedianet.org/papers/om2002/Kidd.om2002.pdf>

2 In 1995, there were eighteen international computer networks in use by activists, such as Peacenet, Labornet, Econet. Gustavo Lins Ribeiro, 'Cybercultural Politics: Political Activism at a Distance in a Transnational World', in Sonia E. Alvarez, Evelina Dagnino and Arturo Escobar (eds), *Cultures of Politics/Politics of Cultures: Re-visioning Latin American Social Movements* (Boulder, CO: Westview Press, 1998).

3 Paul de Armond, 'Netwar in the Emerald City: WTO Protest Strategy and Tactics', in John Arquilla and David Ronfeldt (eds), *Networks and Netwars: The Future of Terror, Crime, and Militancy* (RAND Corporation, 2001), at <www.rand.org/publications/MR/MR1382>

4 Jeff Perlstein, interviewed by Miguel Bocanegra, 'Indymedia: Precursors and Birth', in Notes from Nowhere (ed.), *We are Everywhere: The Irresistible Rise of Global Anticapitalism* (London: Verso, 2003). Interestingly, Perlstein credits Acción Zapatista, from Austin, USA, with bringing these ideas. Austin was also the site of the only US Zapatista Encuentro, in summer 1997, at which the 'media, information, and education' group asserted that 'community development needs to be at the core of our information projects'.

5 Dorothy Kidd, *Carnival and Commons: The Global IMC Network*, Our Media III Conference, Barranquilla, Colombia, May 2003, quoting Armand Mattelart, 1988, and Rafael Roncagliolo, 1992, both at AMARC conferences (World Community Radio Association).

6 In a ten-minute video message created for the Freeing the Media Teach-In, New York City, organized by the Learning Alliance, Paper Tiger TV and FAIR.

7 Kidd, *Carnival and Commons*. Gene Hyde, 'Independent Media Centers: Cyber-Subversion and the Alternative Press', *First Monday*, 7, 4 (April 2002), <www.firstmonday.org/issues/issue7_4/hyde> Also see the reporting from the mainstream: John Tarleton, 'Protesters Develop Their Own Global Internet Service', *Nieman Reports* (Harvard University), 54, 4 (Winter, 2000), pp. 53–5.

8 'Reclaiming the News (a short history of Indymedia UK)', *Squall*, 12 January 2004 at <www.squall.co.uk>

9 Kidd, *Carnival and Commons*.

10 Matthew Arnison, 'Open Publishing is the Same as Free Software', March 2001, June 2003, <www.active.org.au/doc>

11 mh, 13 December 2002, 08:30, see <www.mir.indymedia.org>

12 Maria Suárez Toro, FIRE (Feminist International Radio Endeavor) in Kidd, *Carnival and Commons*.

13 Toro in ibid.

14 Read by Subcomandante Marcos at the First Encuentro for Humanity and Against Neoliberalism, La Realidad, Chiapas, Mexico, August 1996 (at which many internationals were present). Reported in Greg Ruggiero and Kate Duncan, 'Alternative Networks: On the Growing Free Media Movement, Recent Trends in Radical Media Organizing', *Z Magazine*, October 1997.

21 Councils are held in the streets to make decisions (photo by Tim Russo)

21 | Spokes only: reinventing direct democracy

Decisions made by those affected

A hallmark of the movement is direct, participatory democracy. The Zapatistas have repeatedly described to their collaborators the lengthy and thorough meetings used to arrive at their strategies, to formulate their responses to peace offers and to develop community projects. Weekly or even more frequent meetings are held for the purpose of self-governance in each of the communities. When regional decisions are required, a lengthy Consulta is held, in which 'intense discussion in each community is as central to the process as the vote itself'.[1]

Further, the Zapatistas have engaged the entire nation of Mexico in popular plebiscites outside the formal democratic process, so as to be able to answer questions the government does not ask, and in order to establish a direct and dialogic relationship with civil society outside Chiapas. Creative renovations of democratic methods proliferate as movements seek to establish inclusive, participatory and accountable political structures safe from double-crossers and ruses.

Autonomous, direct decision-making is in widespread use: the anti-privatization struggles in Bolivia and Peru both use mass assemblies to determine the course of the struggle,[2] as do the Asembleas in Argentina, the Sem Terra encampments in Brazil, villages resisting dams in Thailand and India, farmers' associations, the unemployed movement in Europe, squats and the blockaded road junctions surrounding meetings like those of the G8 and WTO.

Lead by obeying

In Zapatista communities not every act is taken by collective decision. 'Responsibles' are elected delegates to the councils of the autonomous municipalities. Autonomous collectives also carry out projects. But in keeping with direct democracy, they must 'govern obeying' and are subject to immediate recall if they are not doing so. 'Govern obeying' does not depend on the character or behaviour of the responsibles, but on that of their constitutents who actively '*compel* those governing to carry out their work in accordance with the people's interest, and not in accordance with the interest of a party or of an economic or religious group'.[3] Responsibles are not elites; they do not have power. It is the people who exert the power: 'In that way, if some member of the CCRI does not do their work, if they do not respect the people, "well compa, it is not your place to be there. Then, well, excuse us but we will have to put another in your place."'[4]

Consensus method

Much maligned in the Global North and often inappropriately linked with other practices popular in countercultural movements, elements of consensus process are again in widespread use. The following elements, each of which can be practised with varying intensity, are common methods of democratic process.

- Full participation: The process should facilitate maximum participation, through its technologies as well as its social character, setting and style.
- We are all experts: The process values the perspectives and inputs of *all* affected community members, not only those with previous experience, seniority, education or status.
- If people are upset we don't yet have a good plan: Before taking a decision, dissenting voices are considered carefully. If approval of a proposal is called for and there are votes against, the majority does not 'win'. Instead, a review of the concerns of the minority is undertaken and the proposal is revised. Resulting proposals are considered superior to the original one.
- Stand asides and blocks: Sometimes people are not willing to support a proposal but they do not find it necessary to

oppose it. They may 'stand aside', allowing it to move forwards. If, however, they are very concerned, they may 'block' the proposal, requiring it to be reviewed and changed to address their concerns. A block is very serious for the group, but it is not understood as a sign of division. Instead, it is conceptualized as valuable information about a missing perspective.

- Informal affirmation: Hand gestures and straw polls are used frequently to keep track of the mood of the room on the issue at hand. During discussion, non-verbal responses to speakers balance the speaker's voice with its reception. When dissenters speak up, they and the room see immediately if their concerns are shared.

- Temporary, constrained leadership: Rather than long-term general leaders, the consensus process recognizes temporary leadership with well-defined responsibilities. Leaders will often be defined as 'facilitators', 'coordinators', 'weavers' or 'bottomliners.' Bottomliners invert the prestige or elitism normally associated with leaders; they are the ones who have agreed to do whatever leftover work is necessary to make sure their appointed project is finished on time.

- Commitment to group development: In distributing tasks and responsibilities, those with less experience are favoured for new roles.

- Rotating roles: Leadership tasks such as meeting facilitator are rotated both to develop more group skills and also steadily to shift the power and focus throughout the community.

- Attention to process: Out of concern for non-hegemonic voices and aware of the influence of unstated tensions and conflicts, many groups assign an observer to attend to the process itself. This role empowers the assigned watcher to intervene and innovate when even direct democracy fails to facilitate empowerment and decentre privilege.

Spokes only

Affinity groups

A long-time anarchist method of organizing, affinity groups maximize trust within a small group, enabling members to rely on one another. Called *tertulias*, they have been used for several centuries in Spain. They operate autonomously and are effective at some actions for which a large group would be unwieldy or for which strong connections and collaborative history is useful. Affinity groups obviate the need for conformity to a party line, platform, tactic or march route. They express the movement's commitment to diversity ('one no, many yeses') by allowing for many different ideas and actions to occur simultaneously, maximizing the voice and ingenuity of the larger struggle.

Spokescouncils

Independent affinity groups gather at a non-binding spokescouncil to coordinate their actions, share information and provide support to one another. When it suits their purposes, they may mass up, and they will try not to tread on one another's toes. At a spokescouncil, each group sends one 'spoke' into the centre who maintains good communication with the rest of the group on the outskirts of the meeting. The spoke speaks for the group, but only as directed by them, and checks back often. Individuals without a group may not join the circle of spokes, although they may participate in parts of the meeting.

A spokescouncil is a decision-making body grounded in communities and actions. The spokescouncil limits itself to those decisions that must be made because they affect or require the collaboration of all groups. They generally do not issue manifestos or agree to abstract projects, as diversity is better protected when these functions are done within community groups. Spokescouncils are a vehicle for communication and physical organization of solidarity.

Resources

Anarchism in Action: Methods, Tactics, Skills, and Ideas: <www.radio4all.org/aia>

Collective Book on Collective Process: <www.geocities.com/collectivebook>

Steward Community Woodland consensus process step-by-step: <www.stewardwood.org/resources/DIYconsensus.htm>

Notes

1 These take months and have been a great source of annoyance to the Mexican government, which always wants an answer to its proposals on the spot or within days. From 'The Zapatistas, Anarchism and "Direct Democracy"', *Anarcho-Syndicalist Review*, 27 (Winter 1999).

2 Jordi Martorell, 'Peru – Mass Uprising Defeats Privatisation Plans', *In Defense of Marxism*, 24 June 2002, at <www.marxist.com>

3 Response to question 18, 'Why does the EZLN say it isn't fighting for power?' in 'Subcomandante Marcos Answers 62 Questions from Civil Society', February 2001 (emphasis added). Also see 'The Mexican Zapatistas and Direct Democracy', *Workers Solidarity*, 55, October 1998, online at www.flag.blackened.net/revolt/ws98/ws55_zapatista.html>

4 CCRI member Isacc to *La Jornada*, in 'The Zapatistas, Anarchism and "Direct Democracy"', see note 1.

Spokes only

22 Activists methodically worked in waves of teams to dismantle the fences erected to keep demonstrators out of the WTO 5th Ministerial meetings in Cancún, Mexico, September 2003 (photo by Tim Russo)

22 | Property crime: breaking the spell

Property crime attracts a great deal of criticism. It is accused of delegitimizing and endangering a broader movement. Whether it endangers pacifist colleagues is uncertain, as pacifist events are now attacked by the police with regularity. It is accused of alienating potential allies, none of whom, it is assumed, would be attracted to aggressive acts of resistance.[1] Property crime's message and tactical legitimacy are hotly debated. There are two activist strategies of property crime.

Barricade building and dismantling

Understood as civil disobedience (a moral imperative to break an illegal law), the idea here is that barricades illegally violating freedom of assembly, political voice, democratic participation and freedom of movement are illegal and ought to be dismantled – even at the risk of criminal charges. The most celebrated such event was the dismantling of the fence in Quebec City at the FTAA/ALCA/ZLÉA protests in 2001.

Barricade building is a way of disrupting business, protecting a neighbourhood or an action, and slowing down the police. After months of strikes and protests, resistance to privatization plans in Peru became more intense in June 2002.

> Civil construction workers helped the people to lift the street's cobblestones and use them to build barricades ... The police used tear gas canisters to try to control the demonstrations but finally had to retreat as the mass of people defended themselves with sticks, stones and bottles and managed to maintain control of the city's main square ... Clashes continued throughout the weekend resulting in more than 100 people injured, 52 arrested and damages to property that the government put at $100 million. One student died after being hit directly in the face by a tear gas canister ... On Sunday the

clashes spread to the airport ... where they destroyed equipment in the runway area.[2]

As soon as we reached the Wall ... Pink Silver activists began to attack it ... with steel wheelie bins and tried to clamber up the fence to attach grappling hooks to pull the fence down or make symbolic attempts to reach the top ... us – armed with colourful props and enthusiasm – and the police – armed with guns, water cannon and gas canisters.[3]

Barricade building involves appropriation of public and private property, including cars, and the use of fire. In Argentina, burning tyres are a standard part of road blockades. In Genoa, the creation of barricades and the burning of cars was particularly intense (although some pointed out that the state's fence had already violated neighbourhoods): 'If the cops attack us with everything they have and we need to build barricades, we will make them with whatever is immediately available. We will not sit around in the street trying to figure out whether this or that car are bourgeois or proletarian.'[4]

Challenging private property

Corporate property (banks, ATMs, signage, windows, construction equipment) is attacked, destroyed, re-marked or transformed as part of several strategies.

One is to sabotage corporate outlets to make operations unprofitable. 'While capitalism stalks us as consumers at the same time as dumping us as workers, it has the audacity to squeal when we brick its windows.'[5]

I believe that using the word violent to describe breaking the window of a Nike store takes meaning away from the word. Nike makes shoes out of toxic chemicals in poor countries using exploitative labor practices. Then they sell the shoes for vastly inflated prices to poor black kids from the first world. In my view, this takes resources out of poor communities on both sides of the globe, increasing poverty and suffering ...

What violence does breaking a window at Nike Town

cause? It makes a loud noise; maybe that is what is considered violent. It creates broken glass, which could hurt people, although most of the time those surrounding the window are only Black Bloc protesters who are aware of the risks of broken glass. It costs a giant multi-billion dollar corporation money to replace their window. Is that violent? It is true that some underpaid Nike employee will have to clean up a mess, which is unfortunate, but a local glass installer will get a little extra income too.

A broken window at Nike Town is not threatening to people's safety, but I hope it sends a message that I don't just want Nike to improve their actions, I want them to shut down and I'm not afraid to say it.[6]

Militant groups have used massive, coordinated property crime against particular corporations to compel them to obey social demands, such as recognizing workers' rights, ending animal testing, halting biotechnology field trials or cutting their links with human-rights-violating regimes. These campaigns can include 'proletarian shopping', which politicizes 'looting'.[7]

Sabotage was adopted as a new weapon of struggle for the working class by the General Confederation of Labour in 1897 at the instigation of Émile Pouget. Pouget's *Le Sabotage* argues: 'Sabotage as a form of revolt is as old as human exploitation.' *Le Sabotage*'s American translator affirmed that sabotage 'has nothing to do with violence, neither to life nor to property'. Sabotage was used widely in the anti-apartheid struggle in South Africa during the 1960s. In the last few decades, sabotage has been largely abandoned by labour movements and embraced by environmentalists.

Ecotage is property destruction intended to prevent ecological destruction. It includes acts such as disabling bulldozers, digging up roads and spiking trees, billboard modification, desurveying and road reclamation. Earth First! describes 'monkeywrenching'[8] as 'a step beyond civil disobedience. It is nonviolent, aimed only at inanimate objects ... the deliberate action taken by the Earth defender when all other measures have failed, the process whereby the wilderness defender becomes the wilderness acting in self-defense.'[9] The most widespread current sabotage movement is the uprooting of biotech crops and destruction of biotech seeds, a movement which includes the participation of moderate sectors of agricultural and environmental movements.[10]

A second strategy of property crime is to raise the social costs of an international meeting, such as a WTO Ministerial, so that cities will not want to host such meetings for fear of inflicting costly property crime on corporate friends as well as presenting to the world a temporary image of urban blight.

> Under these circumstances, trashing the town was potentially the best thing to do. The police were too busy protecting the Red Zone, we had effective control of the streets, and this level of destruction will send out an effective message to the whole world, but especially to any other cities that are thinking of hosting summit meetings that if they do then this is what will happen to their city too ... as the *Guardian* reported: 'there is a shortage of cities queueing up to be turned into a war zone'.[11]

It often happens that property crime against shops is systematic in that multinational corporations are attacked and small stores, immigrant shops, etc., are left unharmed. This was the case in Seattle, Gothenburg and Genoa.[12] ' ... very soberly done and thoughtful – walking down the Corso Torino in the aftermath of some of the fighting it was completely clear to see – every single bank was smashed to pieces and *nothing* else was ... Most people involved know very clearly what they are doing and can tell you why.'[13] Not all agree that a distinction should be made between corporate shops and locally owned ones: 'Capitalism is ... a social relation which ... has to do with the fact that wherever we go ... we are confronted with a world of commodities that only money can buy.'[14]

The third, and most interesting, strategy of property crime is as performance art ('working class art')[15] which creates a rupture and 'breaks the spell' of private property.

After n30, people will never see a shop window or a hammer the same way again. The potential uses of an entire cityscape have increased a thousand-fold. Along with the broken windows are the broken spells cast by a corporate hegemony to lull us into forgetfulness of all the violence committed in the name of private property rights and of all the potential of a society without them. Broken windows can be boarded up and replaced but the shattering of assumptions will hopefully persist for some time.[16]

Destroying the boundary which separates public space and need from the private profit machines brings to sudden attention the arbitrary sacredness and legal sanctification of private property while also revealing it as highly vulnerable. The rupture is most often accomplished by graffiti, 'adbusting' (modifying billboards or rearranging the letters in a corporate logo) and breaking windows. The most famous property crime as 'street theatre' was José Bové[17] dismantling a McDonalds in his home town in southern France. About this political action, he says:

We wanted to do this protest in broad daylight, with a large group of people, a non-violent action, but symbolically very strong, and up front with the authorities. We were careful to explain ahead of time to the police that our objective was to dismantle the McDonalds ... Then an officer from the police department called us to say that he was going to ask the manager at McDonalds for a sign of some kind so we could destroy that, that it be more symbolic. We told him: 'Are you kidding? That's nuts. We're going to dismantle the doors and windows.'[18]

Property crime as political protest is not an indication of incipient violence against persons, but a disciplined, intentional strategy of protest in the avowedly non-violent tradition of sabotage. After the May 1998 Geneva WTO protests, 'The convenors replied that they regretted the damage to small shops but that this violence was nothing compared to the violence

215

organized in the WTO building.'[19] In Quebec City, José Bové asserted that 'The first violence is the free market. It's killing people all over the world. And even if some windows go down, that is not violence.'

Nevertheless, militant self-defence (discussed above under 'violence') and property crime function as a 'psychological decolonization', consistent with Frantz Fanon's theory of violence as part of decolonization.[20] Taking control over public space, throwing back tear-gas canisters, freeing colleagues from detention and breaking windows 'breaks the spell'[21] of corporate colonialism and state authority over everyday life.

> Contents of bank files and drawers were scattered about with the ashes, photocopiers were melted, sleek cars were black and crushed ... it seemed as if everyone was totally fascinated and unable to speak ... It's not often that one gets to see what lies behind the sleek machines and walls that run our lives. It was kinda like seeing something you've been taught to respect and fear, become nothing but flimsy garbage.[22]

Notes

1 For example, in the USA, many African American and Latino youth choose an aggressive form of resistance to the occupation of their communities. The gang phenomenon in communities of colour has always been explicitly linked to political resistance. According to Christian Parenti, the youth who choose such a path are the inheritors of a militant tradition. They are 'the impoverished low-wage working class and unemployed youth who have fallen below the statistical radar, but whose spirits are not broken and whose expectations for a decent life and social inclusion are dangerously alive and well' (*Lockdown America: Police and Prisons in the Age of Crisis* [London: Verso, 1999], p. 46).

2 Jordi Martorell, 'Peru – Mass Uprising Defeats Privatisation Plans', *In Defense of Marxism*, 24 June 2002, at <www.marxist. com>

3 Linden Farrer, 'Dance Around the G8: Pink Silver, Pink, and Silver: Contested Identities Against the G8', 2002. Dissertation summary at <www.pcworks.demon.co.uk/magazine/campaign/pinksilver.htm>

4 K, 'Being Black Block', pp. 31–5 in *On Fire: The Battle of Genoa and the Anti-capitalist Movement* (London: One-off Press, 2001), p. 33.

5 Jazz, 'The Tracks of Our Tears', pp. 80–99 in ibid., pp. 99, 98.

6 Mary Black, 'Letter from Inside the Black Bloc', *AlterNet*, 25 July 2001.

7 George Katsiaficas, *The Subversion of Politics: European Autonomous Social Movements and the Decolonization of Everyday Life* (New Jersey: Humanities Press, 1997), p. 137.

8 Edward Abbey is credited with conceptualizing 'monkey-wrenching' in his 1975 book *The Monkey Wrench Gang* (Salt Lake City, UT: Dream Garden Press, 1975, 1985) and the practice has been taken up by international groups such as the Animal Liberation Front, Earth Liberation Front and Earth First!

9 <www.earthfirstjournal.org/efj/primer/Monkeywrench.html>

10 While there are constant reports of such attacks all over the world, I was unable to find an international compilation quantifying these actions. An archive is kept at <www.tao.ca/~ban/ar.htm>

11 Anonymous, 'Being Busy', pp. 41–54 in *On Fire*, p. 50.

12 REVO eyewitness account, 'Sweden: In the Front Line in Gothenberg', *Workers Power Global Week*, 52, E-newswire of the LRCI, 22 June 2001, at <www.workerspower.com>

13 Anonymous, 'Being Busy', in *On Fire*, p. 49.

14 K, 'Being Black Block', in ibid., p. 33.

15 Jazz, 'The Tracks of Our Tears', in ibid., p. 96.

16 Communiqué published by one section of the Seattle n30 Black Bloc, *Do or Die*, 9.

17 Asked his impressions of Seattle n30, Bové described the protests as 'Absolutely non-violent. Nothing happened in Seattle … There was no real damage, nothing more than what would happen at a Confédération rally in France in Montauban' ('A World Struggle is Underway', interview with José Bové by Lynn Jeffress with Jean-Paul Mayanobe, *Z Magazine*, June 2001) <www.zmag.org/ZMag/articles/june01bove.htm>

18 Ibid.

19 PGA Bulletin, 'Peoples' Global Action Against "Free" Trade and the WTO', 2 (June 1998), at <www.agp.org>

20 Frantz Fanon, 'Concerning Violence', in *The Wretched of the Earth* (New York: Grove Press, 1961, 1968).

21 *Breaking the Spell* is a PickAxe movie about the Seattle WTO n30 protests, available at <www.crimethinc.com/a/fmp>

22 Brian S., 'Reporting from the Frontline', pp. 17–22 in *On Fire*, p. 18.

23 | Diversity of tactics

In North America, after Seattle, an extensive debate took place among activists about the legitimacy of property crime and how to practise respect for diversity of tactics. This debate became more refined over time, with the careful development of 'action guidelines' and 'zones'.

The evolving framework 'diversity of tactics' was developed to accord equal respect to candlelight vigils, property crime, permitted marches and everything in between. Because it protects space for property crime, diversity of tactics is sometimes mistakenly interpreted as being supportive of or synonymous with it.

Action guidelines

In preparation for a protest, the spokescouncil will agree to 'action guidelines'. It is in this process that solidarity is initially established. Action guidelines for the 2000 Washington DC protests (a16) were: '1. We will use no violence, physical or verbal, towards any person. 2. We will carry no weapons. 3. We will not bring or use any alcohol or illegal drugs. 4. We will not destroy property (excepting barricades erected to prevent us from exercising our rights).'

Two years later, the politics of solidarity had evolved to include 'unity' agreements, meaning specifically that pacifist protesters will not report or otherwise draw attention to activists using property crime tactics. Action guidelines for the September 2002 IMF/WB protests were '1. Separation between permitted and non-permitted events by time and space to insure safe space for internationals, high risk folks or others who want to be assured of avoiding police repression in any form. 2. Cultivation of a sense of unity between all aspects of the action whether permitted or non-permitted.'

Action guidelines are scrupulously adhered to by the vast

23 The large pink pig eating the world was part of street theatre. The seated people are in a lockdown, blocking the street (photo by Tim Russo)

majority of activists. They do not, however, make their way to those who join in spontaneously, independent of the careful organizing procedures. Nevertheless, there have been few convictions of protesters for actions that violated the guidelines.

Some blocs create guidelines to protect diversity of tactics within the bloc while also maintaining unity. An example of this is the Pink Silver bloc for the G8 protests in Genoa.

> The working paper produced for the group stated that there should be 'no intention to create violent confrontation with the police (no pro-active use of stones, molotovs, etc.)'. This is basically a statement of non-violence – an attempt to prevent violence, but worded in a way that allowed participants to respond to violence as they felt fit and as the situation dictated.[1]

Coloured zones

As part of 'diversity of tactics' there have also been attempts to separate (in space and/or time) actions involving different levels of 'risk' while also maintaining a united front of solidarity among activists and organizations with divergent beliefs about tactics.

The separation is achieved through colour-coded zones. 'Green' zones host 'safe' activities which are supposed to run no risk of arrest or police attack (either because they involve only legal activities or because they have state permits). These are areas and activities considered safe for children, elders, immigrants and other vulnerable people.

'Yellow' hosts civil disobedience and non-violent direct action which, depending on the situation, could result in arrest or police attack, but which also could end up being safe.

'Red' zones demarcate actions expected to result in police attention. These could include property crime, trying to cross police lines, or non-violent direct actions (such as a lockdown in a particularly important area). Since planned red actions are more secretive and might be organized with a small affinity group, participants might also be more vulnerable simply because fewer people will be around. Red zones are rarely announced in advance and often move around with particular groups, but they have a territorial mandate, which is to employ themselves far from the pre-established, mapped and well-advertised green zones.

After Quebec City, where diversity of tactics included 'permanent' green zones soon awash with tear-gas and eventually invaded by police, and where yellow ceased to have any meaning, it seemed that red actions make it impossible for yellow or green actions to take place at all. While militant activists are responsive to concerns about 'safety', they also remind other activists that the police will attack *any* kind of action which they perceive as a threat (even pacifist ones), and that militants' frequent defence of pacific actions is more significant than their role in stimulating police violence.

In New York for WEF there was an increased awareness of the relationships between areas and actions. We used the phrases 'yellowish-green' and 'greenish-yellow', and talked at length about how to effect a transition from a 'green day' to a 'yellow night' while making sure to inform people fully. At the last minute, a spontaneous spokescouncil halted this transition entirely due to the presence of children and other 'unarrestables'[2] who were trapped by police barricades in the area that was supposed to 'turn yellow'.

Lines

At European actions, it is common for several distinct 'lines' to move at once. These allow for clear invitations to different tactical preferences. Independent organization of lines is made possible by the significant number of militants, often in several tactical flavours. In the USA and Canada, militant sectors are often sufficiently small that if they make an independent approach they are easily contained and isolated. In Miami in 2003, one such group, targeted for containing a high percentage of black-clad folks, was captured by an encirclement of bicycle-wielding police, penned, and held until other actions were over, then released in even smaller groups, some of which were then jumped, brutalized and arrested.

RANT Collective 'Solidarity in Practice for the Street Demonstrations'

We are very different groups. We are not necessarily immediate allies nor are we each other's greatest enemy. There are many things on which we do not agree. But, we will be in the streets together to protest this war. We know that the police and media are trying to divide us in order to crush our movements. Solidarity is the way in which our diversity becomes our strength, we build our movements and we protect each other's bodies, lives and rights.

We believe we have some things in common. We believe in basic human rights and the need to live with respect and dignity. We believe we must protect this planet – our air, water, earth and food or we will all die. We believe these global corporate and political institutions are serving only the interests of the rich. We all agree it's time for fundamental and radical change.

As we take to the streets together, let us work to be in solidarity with one another. The following suggestions offer ways in which we can make our solidarity real.

Personal: Challenge and critique other groups and individuals in constructive ways and in a spirit of respect ... Don't make assumptions no matter what a person looks like or what groups they belong to. Don't assume tactics are the only way to measure militancy or radicalness. Refrain from personal attacks, even on people with whom we strongly disagree ... Understand that even though we may disagree we have come to our politics, strategies and choice of tactics through thoughtful and intelligent consideration of issues, circumstances and experiences.

Street: Do not intentionally put people at risk who have not chosen it. Do not turn people over to the police. Do not let people within our own groups interfere with other groups. Respect the work of all medics, legal observers, independent media people. Share food, water, medical and other supplies. Support everyone who is hurt, gassed, shot or beaten. Respect other groups' rights to do a certain type of protest at certain times and places. If you choose to participate, do so within the tone and tactics they set. If you do not agree, do not participate in that protest or bring another protest into that time and space. Understand that our actions and tactics have repercussions that go beyond ourselves and our immediate groups. And that some tactics overrun the space of others. If you choose to negotiate with the police, never do so for other groups of which you are not a part.

Media: Do not denounce other demonstrators. Talk about your strategy, not others'. Acknowledge other groups' existence and role they play in creating change. Acknowledge that we sometimes disagree about strategy and tactics. Avoid using the word violence. Condemn police repression and brutality. Share media contacts and do not monopolize the media's attention.

Jail solidarity: No one is free until everybody is free.

Source: Based on a dialogue in DC, summer 2001.

Safety and solidarity

Commenting on Genoa, US activist Starhawk rejects the attempt to protect moderate protesters or adhere to a non-consensual vision of 'legitimacy' by condemning militance:

I no longer see any place of safety. Or rather, I see that in the long run our safest course is to act strongly now ... In a life or death situation, there's a great temptation to attempt to exert more control, to set rules, to police each other, to retreat to what seems like safe ground ... Agreements are only agreements when everyone participates in making them. If one wing of the movement attempts to impose them, they are not agreements, but decrees, and moreover, decrees that will not be respected and that we have no power to enforce ... We have a right to ask for solidarity from everyone who wants to be out on the street together.[3]

The 'street solidarity' statement in the box on pp. 223–4 was developed by a diverse North American consortium including both militants and pacifists. It is one of many such statements which will be developed as people work to express solidarity while respecting diversity.

Notes

1 Linden Farrer, 'Dance Around the G8: Pink Silver, Pink, and Silver: Contested Identities Against the G8', 2002. Dissertation summary at <www.pcworks.demon.co.uk/magazine/campaign/pinksilver.htm>

2 The term 'arrestable' refers to people who are prepared to be arrested at a given action. 'Unarrestable' refers to people who would face particular hardships if arrested, such as transgender people, people on probation, immigrants without legal status, or people who would face life sentences upon another conviction, even for a minor sentence.

3 Starhawk, 'Staying on the Streets', pp. 125–34 in *On Fire: The Battle of Genoa and the Anti-capitalist Movement* (London: One-off Press, 2001), pp. 128–33.

24 Black Bloc on the move with mobile defence
(photo by Tim Russo)

24 | Black Bloc

The image of the Northern anti-globalization movement has been frozen as a masked youth pursuing some obscure and apparently violent purpose. Despite their rather small part in the global movement, this imagery often displaces the struggles of the Global South in the Northern imaginary. Fear and judgement within as well as outside the movement focus debate on broken windows, garbage-can fires and militant self-defence during police riots rather than on the far more substantive and devastating impacts of neoliberal policies.

What is a Black Bloc?

The key thing to understand about Black Bloc is that it is a *tactic*, not an organization. Each Black Bloc is a temporary collaboration lasting a few days at most. A number of small affinity groups mass up as a Black Bloc for a particular manifestation. They organize to create a large group to coordinate their actions and to provide safety in numbers and protection through mutual aid. Black Blocs do not create ideological platforms, only action frameworks in context.

Although Black Blocs do not take up arms, they do at times engage in self-defence, property crime, attempt to breach police barriers and express a militant culture. They participate in non-violent and even pacifist actions, provide direct services, and protect other protesters.

> The Black Bloc is no bullshit. It should not be trivially associated with vandalism and irrational devastation ... As the recent history of the movement proves, the Black Bloc are not static and can adopt different tactics and seek 'cross-fertilization' ... Moreover, they are more fanciful than people think: a few months ago Black Blocsters split off a demo ... entered a destitute neighborhood and picked up garbage. When journalists

asked what the fuck they were doing, they answered: 'You wrote that we would trash the town, we decided to pick up the trash!'[1]

Black Blocs have been organized and perceived quite differently at different actions. In DC in April 2000 (a16), the bloc primarily acted in defence of other protesters (often unprepared for police violence), and were greeted with cheers. In Quebec in April 2001, the Black Bloc assertively breached Canada's 'wall of shame', a massive fence surrounding the meetings. 'It was there that the bloc as tactic, in pulling the widely unpopular fence down, really connected with the feeling of the march, and many in the city as a whole.'[2] In Prague in September 2000, they mounted the most aggressive actions in trying to battle police. They wore and carried some defensive shielding and hurled cobblestones in an effort to break through police lines to the convention centre. In Gothenburg in June 2001 the Black Bloc staged a riot in order to expose the government's latest attempt to coopt dissent. In Genoa in July 2001, they were blamed for bringing on police violence and for harbouring police provocateurs.

> The point about the Black Bloc is that people simply want the autonomy to be able to express their anger as they see fit.[3]

> It is impossible at this point to form a radical activist group without the fear of infiltration and disruption by the police and, for some, taking militant direct action in the streets with very little planning and working only with small networks of friends are the only meaningful forms of protest available.[4]

Who is in a Black Bloc?

Claiming that anarchists and Black Bloc are the same is completely inaccurate.

> Although most anarchists would never wear black bandanas over their faces or break windows at McDonalds, almost all of us are anarchists. Most folks I know who have used Black Bloc tactics have day jobs working for nonprofits ... Some don't

have full-time jobs, but instead spend most of their time working for change in their communities ... if they did not have
radical political and social agendas, [they] would be compared
with nuns, monks, and others who live their lives in service ...
I think that the stereotype is correct that we are mostly young
and mostly white, although I wouldn't agree that we are mostly
men.[5]

In Europe, it is usually not just the Black Bloc which is a bloc –
everyone is in blocs. A normal leftie demo on the continent will
be composed of all the various parties and unions arranged in
blocs, one after the other, each marching in a group behind
their banner. It is normal for the anarchists (whether by choice
or compulsion is unclear) to bring up the rear of the march,
forming a Black Bloc at the end of the demo, often trashing
things along the route of the march or fighting the police ...
[in Genoa] there were lots of anarchists who were not in the
Black Bloc and lots of people in the Black Bloc who were not
anarchists ... I saw people from the Kurdistan Workers Party
and Basque nationalists in with the Black Bloc.[6]

Relations with other groups

Black Blocs act in staunch support of all other demonstrators as appropriate – whether this means physical defence or
silent pacifist accompaniment – and ask for the same solidarity
in return. Unfortunately, what they often get as thanks for their
solidarity is to be turned over to the police or media, alienated
from the movement, vilified as provocateurs, detractors, or
dangers or blamed for harbouring infiltrators.

The mainstream media's current consensus is that the Black
Bloc is bad and extremely dangerous. The progressive media's
most common line is that the Black Bloc is bad, but at least
there aren't many of us ... The biggest complaint that the left
has expressed about the Black Bloc is that we make the rest
of the protesters look bad. It is understandably frustrating for
organizers who have spent months planning a demonstration
when a group of scary looking young people get all of the news

coverage by lighting things on fire. Yet what is missing in this critique is an acknowledgement that the corporate media never covers the real content of demonstrations.[7]

We're witnessing a very serious attempt at criminalizing this section of the movement. We refuse to save our ass to the detriment of the Black Bloc, we regard them as a fully legitimate part of the movement and refuse any distinction between 'good protesters' and 'bad protesters'.[8]

Militancy

Scholar George Katsiaficas points out that it was the development of militance and spontaneity in political culture which, although a small part of the larger progressive movements, influenced the entire First World movement significantly. Referring to their role in the 1988 IMF/World Bank protests in Berlin, he writes that 'the initiative of the Autonomen' with anti-imperialist analysis and wearing helmets 'resulted in larger actions, and they were the militant organizers creating a context in which other forms of participation ... had meaning'.[9] 'The in-yer-face, on the streets anti-capitalism is what gives our movement its vitality and attracts support for our activities – it's not something to be played down, disguised or be embarrassed about.'[10]

Sometimes as part of clandestinity and sometimes simply in fear of infiltrators, Black Blocs practise 'security culture'. Unfriendly at best, this culture can contribute to the isolation of militants. Katsiaficas maps the difficulties which militance causes for organizers. His studies reveal a 'stark subcycle within the better-known synergistic dynamic of repression and resistance: secretive conspiratorial resistance helps minimize the possibility and impact of open popular forms of resistance; guerrilla actions replace massive mobilizations; and the impetus to increasing democracy is lost as the bitterness of confrontation becomes primary.' Describing one militant group, he writes: 'In the process, it has repeatedly exhibited disdain for legal methods of struggle and set a standard of "commitment" that essentially invoked its own members' deaths as a superior form of political activism when compared with others whose risks are not as extreme.'[11] He argues that this hierarchy enables 'the forces of order [to] thrive while popular movements become weakened and vulnerable'. Scholar Donatella della Porta points out that clandestinity absorbs an expanding portion of resources while inducing spiralling insularity and elitism.[12]

Katsiaficas's documentation and analysis seem to suggest that, in the long term, when militance is well-integrated into large public confrontations, it is empowering and radicalizing to the larger movements, but when secretive, it isolates the group and weakens the movement. Campaigns involving secretive and militant actions may be both effective and less damaging to organizations if they are short-term. Militance at demos increases their disruptive power.[13]

> On demonstrations like these there are two main factors that are constantly argued over – militancy and numbers. One group of people are worried that certain levels of militancy will reduce the numbers on protests, and the others are worried that large numbers mean nothing if no-one does anything.[14]

> A further complication in the dynamic of the anti-globalization mobilizations is that objectively it is the militancy of the *casseurs* that have created the real problem for the authorities. The capitalist institutions under attack can quite successfully barricade themselves in, but it is not acceptable to the state that the Black Bloc reduce the whole city to rubble outside, stealing the agenda in the media as well.[15]

Resources

David and X, *The Black Bloc Papers* (Black Clover Press, printed by Insubordinate Editions, a project of the Claustrophobia Collective, Baltimore, MD, available through AK Press, 2002).

On Fire: The Battle of Genoa and the Anti-capitalist Movement (London: One-off Press, 2001).

Black Bloc

Notes

1 White Overalls of Bologna and the Wu Ming collective, 'Stop the Encirclement of the Black Bloc', 19 June 2001; <www.wumingfoundation.com/english/giap/mysterytours.html>

2 '"Anti-capitalism" as Ideology ... and as Movement?', *Aufheben,* 10 (Autumn 2001), <www.geocities.com/aufheben2/index.html>

3 Anonymous, 'Being Busy', pp. 41–54 in *On Fire: The Battle of Genoa and the Anti-capitalist Movement* (London: One-off Press, 2001), p. 46.

4 Mary Black, 'Letter from Inside the Black Bloc', *AlterNet,* 25 July 2001, <www.alternet.org>

5 Ibid.

6 Anonymous, 'Being Busy', p. 44.

7 Black, 'Letter from Inside the Black Bloc'.

8 White Overalls of Bologna and the Wu Ming collective, 'Stop the Encirclement of the Black Bloc', <www.wumingfoundation.com.english/giap/mysterytour>

9 George Katsiaficas, *The Subversion of Politics: European Autonomous Social Movements and the Decolonization of Everyday Life* (New Jersey: Humanities Press, 1997), p. 131.

10 Tommy, 'Trots and Liberals', pp. 104–8 in *On Fire*, p. 105.

11 Katsiaficas, *The Subversion of Politics*, pp. 131–2.

12 Donatella della Porta, *Social Movements, Political Violence, and the State* (Cambridge: Cambridge University Press, 1995).

13 Frances Fox Piven and Richard Cloward, *Poor People's Movements: Why They Succeed, How They Fail* (New York: Vintage, 1978).

14 Anonymous, 'Being Busy', p. 53.

15 '"Anti-capitalism" as Ideology ... and as Movement?'.

25 | Tute Bianche: citizenship of the absurd

The tactic of Tute Bianche understands itself as a manifestation of Zapatismo – expressing fierceness which avoids violence, radicalism which does not seek to take the state, politics beyond ideologies, and providing a face for the invisible. Its intention to put into practice Zapatismo in different contexts is one of many such experiments. Politically, Tute Bianche blocs are generally aligned with immigration rights, prisoners, marginalized radicals (including communists and anarchists) and 'everyone else made invisible by the free market'.[1]

Like other tactics, Tute Bianche is not a standing organization with members. Persons from many groups participate in the Tute Bianche tactic on demos. Tute Bianche was begun in Italy and has been used in many other countries. For the Genoa G8 protests in July 2001, the Tute Bianche bloc had 20,000 people from several countries, including a strong UK contingent identified as Wombles.

The Tute Bianche tactic involves a group which stays tightly together while wearing personal body armour made of household products such as cardboard, foam and empty plastic water bottles. Over the armour, many wear white painter's overalls and life-jackets, resulting in a comic bulky look. They carry collective shielding such as massive rafts of balloons and inner tubes. They approach the police lines ponderously, stop and announce their intention, as citizens, to pass 'with arms up'[2] peacefully through the police lines to attend the meetings, and then push against the police, producing comic mayhem.

> For years our practice of self-defence has been instrumentalised by the media. Every time the police charged a legitimate and peaceful march or demonstration, it was always the fault of 'the autonomists' ... We decided to send strong images and signals that left no doubts as to intentions.

25 upper: The Ya Basta! Brigade prepares its
home-made armour to take on the Czech police
at the IMF/World Bank meetings in Prague. They
led their brigade with a banner painted with
a Zapatista rebel statement, *Todo para todos*
(Everything for Everyone) (September, 2000)
(photo by Tim Russo) lower: 'A group of people
organised in the tortoise-shaped "testudo"
formation ... wearing white overalls and carrying
plexiglass shields ... the demonstrators disobey, at
their own physical risk, shouting ironic slogans ...
the EZLN battle cry "Zapata, vive, la lucha sigue",
frequently fills the air ... The rebels ask for free
access to the fortress of the OECD Summit ... The
"testudo" advances a little ... the cry "Freedom,
Freedom" is almost in contact with the police lines
now ... Neoliberalism is now naked' (Ya Basta,
Milano, Italy: OECD Bologna 15 June 2000) (photo
from Peoples' Global Action)

So we invented ... All things that were visible and clearly for defensive purposes only. We wanted people to understand on which side lay reason, and who had started the violence. When we decide to disobey the rules imposed by the bosses of neo-liberalism, we do it by putting our bodies on the line, full stop. People can see images ... that can't be manipulated: a mountain of bodies that advances, seeking the least harm possible to itself, against the violent defenders of an order that produces wars and misery. And the results are visible, people understand this, the journalists can't invent lies that contradict the images; last but not least, the batons bounce off the padding.[3]

Luca, a spokesperson for the Tute Bianche, states: 'We want to show that it is possible to rebel against the order using our bodies as weapons.'[4] One of the training manuals in circulation is entitled *BodyHammer*. Describing the tactic as 'biopolitics' and citing Foucault, the Tute Bianche sees itself as 'a new form of opposition to power'.

The Tute Bianche tactic has succeeded in overcoming police and entering a detention facility (via Corelli, Milan, January 2000), with the result that the press was able to follow them in and document the concentration-camp conditions. The exposure led to the closure of the facility. A successful Tute Bianche assault on a biotech conference in Genoa (Mobilitebio, May 2000) closed it down, and this event was followed shortly by townships, and the country, renouncing GMOs.

The humorous (yet effective!) tactic draws on European traditions of dada, surrealism and the absurd. A call to action for the June 2000 Bologna protests stated: 'The program foresees actions in every street and square to disturb, *turn into ridicule* and block the OECD summit.'[5]

In addition to effective invasions and a re-enlivening of political discourse, the tactic draws attention to issues of citizenship in a context of state violence. Defensive use of the body is criminalized by the state and attacked. This event draws attention simultaneously to the impoverishment of citizenship

'A Busload of Lies Exposed', July 2001

The White Overalls are not a movement, they are a tool which was devised in the context of a broader movement (the *Social Centers* of the Charta of Milan) and made available to an even broader movement (the global one). Nowadays the white overalls exist in many countries ...

Anybody can wear the white overall as long as they respect the white overall's *style*, which entails a practical refusal of the violence/non-violence dichotomy, a constant reference to Zapatism, a detachment from most XXth-century experiences and the awareness of how important symbols are ...

The white overall ... hasn't got militaristic origins: back in Autumn 1994 the Mayor of Milan evicted the Leoncavallo squatted centre and stated: 'Squatters are nothing other than ghosts now!' His description was accepted ironically, and thousands of people dressed in white stormed the streets of the city and rioted for hours. That was the real debut of the white overalls, and it wasn't a 'fluffy' one ... After that debut, the imagery of the white overall was enriched by ironic references to the 'blue overalls' [tute blu, the Italian equivalent of 'blue collars']: nowadays labour has changed, in the northern hemisphere 'flexibility', part-time and precarious jobs have made exploitation less visible, there's a new 'ghostly' working class. The white overall is a practical joke ...

The white overall is not an identity, it is a tool. One shouldn't even say 'I'm a white overall', the correct phrase should be: 'I wear a white overall'. The people wearing the white overall are funny and ridiculous, they look like the tyre man in the Michelin logo. The people wearing the white overall burst into laughter when they see each other, and when the cops charge they can't run away (after all, they 'dress up' in order NOT to run away), and they're an easy target, like a cow in a lobby. The semi-

> official salute of the people who wear the white overall is ridiculous as well (a fist with the little finger raised) ...
>
> The people who wear the white overall are consciously ridiculous, and that's the point. When they cease to be funny, the movement will need another tool. Anyway, things are working fine so far ...
>
> *Source*: <www.nadir.org/nadir/initiativ/agp/free/genova/busload.htm>

and to the essential violence of the policies and institutions being confronted – particularly of those which claim to be 'democratic'. 'We are acting as citizens, putting our persons at risk, in order to demonstrate that the democracy of the IMF and the World Bank is tanks and armed police.'[6]

Resources

Italian website: <www.tutebianche.org>

Tute Bianche pages at PGA: <www.nadir.org/nadir/initiativ/agp/free/tute/index.htm>

UK Wombles (use white overalls and other tactics): <www.wombles.org.uk>

Sarin, *Body Hammer: Tactics and Self-Defense for the Modern Protester*, at <www.devo.com/sarin/bodyhammer.html>

Ya Basta!: <www.yabasta.it>

Invisibles-Madrid: <www.nodo50.org/invisibles>

Notes

1 Giorgio, a member of Ya Basta from Rome, quoted in the *Guardian*, 19 July 2001.

2 Prague Indymedia Center, *Praha 2000* (documentary film), <praguevideo.indymedia.org>

3 'Changing the World (One Bridge at a Time)? Ya Basta after Prague', Steve Wright talks with Hobo from Radio Sherwood (<www.sherwood.it>), a media project that is closely linked to Ya Basta. Uploaded 28 October 2000. <www.geocities.com/swervedc/yabasta.html>

4 Jesús Ramírez Cuevas, 'The Body as a Weapon for Civil Disobedience', *La Jornada*, 15 October 2000.

5 <www.nadir.org/nadir/initiativ/agp/free/tute/genua.htm#Bologna> (my emphasis).

6 Jesús Ramírez Cuevas, 'The Body as a Weapon for Civil Disobedience', 15 October 2000.

26 | Tactical frivolity: why we dance

Pink Silver is a manifestation of the carnivalesque Reclaim
the Streets approach to protest, described as 'tactical frivolity'. Participants wear extravagant costumes, organize amateur
samba bands, express a distinctly queer aesthetic, and invoke
surrealist absurdity as a political critique. Pink silver has several theoretical components: feminism, a political space which
rejects dichotomies, and frivolity.

Feminism

The original Prague Pink Silver bloc was organized by a
group of women from the UK.

> Their idea: to dress up in outrageous costumes – half Baccha-
> nalian ball-gown, half Rio carnival dancer – and confront the
> police, unmasked, and armed only with feminism and feather
> dusters ... By exposing their vulnerability, dancing and sing-
> ing, and generally being silly, they not only subverted the idea
> of confrontation, but also demanded that the police see them
> as human beings.

One of the participants explained: 'Doing an action in a carnival
costume ... For women, facing all-male riot police, it is a way
of exploiting our vulnerability, making them see that we're
people, not just things to be hit. We all got hit anyway.'[1]

Implicit in the imagery and vision of Pink Silver is a queer
gender aesthetic, which draws on drag imagery, queer high
femme, riot grrrl and glam feminism as well as gender-bending
for pink-clad men.

The US group Code Pink, although quite different from Pink
Silver, does share the use of feminism and absurdity. Their
name was created as a riff on the Bush administration's colour-
coded 'homeland security' system. They issue their own alerts,
warning that the policies of empire are a threat to women and

26 Infernal Noise Brigade <www.infernalnoise.
org> (photo by Tim Russo)

peace everywhere. A pacifist group, unlike the non-violent Pink Silver, Code Pink organizes pink vigils and legal pink banner hangs, although its eighty chapters develop their actions autonomously and some have included invasions of meetings in pink formal-wear. Code Pink also operates outside the USA.

Political space rejecting dichotomies

In Europe, ideological debates between groups were already tiresome before the emergence of the alterglobalization movement. Tute Bianche and Pink Silver are among those creating a new ideological perspective. Pink Silver tends to use anarchist methods of organizing but does not sloganize (in fact, the 'proposed definition of pink' for Genoa stated 'no trademarks/no logos/no organizatorial labels') and is therefore equally friendly with socialists, communists and peace groups. Pink Silver and Tute Bianche also defend other groups (both physically and rhetorically), hoping for solidarity in return.

At manifestations, some groups and organizations act together only after a long and painful process of formulating an ideological position and settling on appropriate tactics. Other groups, sometimes with a great deal less bickering, worry less about the particular message than its general delivery, joining with other groups around the tactics they see to be most useful in that particular context or manifestation. Black Bloc, Tute Bianche and Pink Silver are the beginnings of a tactical grammar. This is not to say that ideology has been abandoned entirely; the participants in the blocs have a great deal in common. Strategically, Pink Silver rejects the spikey vs. fluffy debates and embraces a diversity of tactics within the group.

The pacifists appropriated the colour pink and referred to the group as the 'Pink' group. Those who wanted to be able to respond to situations as they arose identified with the colour silver and referred to it as 'Pink Silver' ... The division between the factions appeared to centre primarily on the level of experience of street demonstrations ... The 'silvers' ... were largely from Europe; the 'pinks' were made up primarily of

P ! N k A n D S ! L V 3 R FOR AN ANTI-G8
BLOC/kade in Lausanne and Elsewhere
(2003)

To anarchists not Black, socialists not Red and ecologists not Green.

We invite you to join us in creating a PINK AND SILVER political and tactical space ... We understand the heart of Pink and Silver as 'tactical frivolity': a creative, joyous, diverse, fluid and life-affirming form of direct action and civil disobedience. A self-organized mongrel of party and protest, based on values such as autonomy, solidarity, diversity, initiative, indiscipline and mutual aid. Pink and Silver has both soft and hard edges, depending only on what you make of it, although they are usually both present in action and people can frolic from one to the other ... But you will always know Pink and Silver when you see it, because it is so, SO Pink and Silver. It's so Pink and Silver that anyone who has done it before begins to smile just talking about it – and this is scientifically proven.

We want to help shut down the G8 summit ... And at least for a moment, on the morning of Sunday J1, after we have put out the fires around the lake and put on our armour (costumes and dreams) and weapons (feather-dusters and samba), we want their eyes to squint at the sunrise of our freedom.

What exactly we will do is something that we can only decide together ... We want to do this in a collective structure based on affinity groups, one that cherishes decentralization and autonomy alongside solidarity and coordination. A bunch of us are going to try to facilitate the creation of such a structure in Lausanne, and if other people and affinity groups want to do the same in Geneva, or anywhere else, that will be so fantastic we can't even describe it. <g8illegal.lautre.net>

North American and Israeli activists. There was no discernible gender divide between the two positions, just a geographical one.[2]

When faced with tactical disagreements, Pink Silver's response is to refine a framework of inclusion. In Genoa, that meant juggling with times and locations. If the scene became 'violent', the Silvers were to separate themselves from the Pinks so both could pursue their preferred response. Until then, they would not let their spikey vs. fluffy differences get in the way of the dancing. They also reject a hierarchy of confrontations. 'Pink & Silver is the opposite of individualized macho militancy.' In feminist style, fears are addressed collectively, and empowerment depends on the fact that the 'confrontational level' is 'determined by ourselves', not by an absolutist party line.[3]

Frivolity

Frivolity accomplishes several goals: fun, creativity, a social rupture and a substantive message.

Pink Silver presents itself in contrast to the boring and rigid politics of 'mass-produced banners and regulated marches' (favoured by trade unions and NGOs).[4] As Reclaim the Streets, the tactic creates 'roving street party carnivals with samba bands instead of sound systems ... Pink Silver aimed to be a prominent carnivalesque spectacle. It was to be colourful, noticeable, fun to watch and empowering to be a part of.'[5]

Frivolity provides a space for the imagination of participants and observers and encourages them to create their own costumes in what Farrer calls a DIY (do-it-yourself) manner which does not require great courage or training. 'Anyone can play an instrument, make props, or cover themselves in glitter, and show their feelings that way.'[6] The tactic is inviting and accessible.

According to a Pink Silver website, this approach 'attracts attention and puts into uncertainty cops, the media, and the public, thus being an interesting form of communication guerrilla'.[7] Perhaps most revealing of the way in which tactical frivolity has created new space is the gleefully retold tale of the Toronto police who, when confronted by a festive Reclaim the Streets-type event, reported over the radio: 'This is not a protest. Repeat. This is not a protest. This is some kind of artistic impression. Over.'[8]

What does frivolity communicate? A 'stark contrast ... diametrically opposed to capitalist economics which force homogeneity on the world'.[9] 'This movement ... shows the limits of an economic accounting – not with recalculated sums but with carnival – in order to reveal those things that do not show up as losses on the balance sheet: nature, people, culture, and lost souls.'[10]

Black, white and pink do not represent the whole range of tactics practised at street protests. The tactical grammar is adapted to specific political contexts and action goals. An emphasis on humour and absurdity is not confined to the Tute Bianche and Pink Silver. The movement as a whole has great enthusiasm for satire, which appears in street theatre, pranks and culture jams. In Prague, even the Black Bloc brought a 10-foot diameter beach ball for 'playing' in the spray from the water cannon. (It bore the phrase 'balls to the IMF' and served nicely as a shield.) Nor are the tactics of stone-throwing confined to the Black Bloc. When provoked, members of Tute Bianche have also engaged in hurling projectiles, despite some attempts to maintain discipline. Many activists point out that it doesn't much matter which tactics you choose. In Prague and Genoa, all three lines were violently attacked by police.

Resources

Linden Farrer, 'Dance Around the G8: Pink Silver, Pink, and Silver: Contested Identities Against the G8', 2002. Dissertation summary at <www.pcworks.demon.co.uk/magazine/campaign/pinksilver.htm>

Dark Star (ed.), *Beneath the Paving Stones: Situationists and the Beach* (Oakland, CA: AK Press, 2001).

Pink & Silver index page: <www.antenna.nl/organicchaos/PinkSilver/PSindex.html>

The drum band referred to as 'Samba band' associated with Pink & Silver: <www.rhythmsofresistance.co.uk>

Pink & Silver: Advertisement Video: available from <trojan@nadir. org>

Notes

1 Notes from Nowhere and Kate Evans, 'It's Got to be Silver and Pink: On the Road with Tactical Frivolity', pp. 290–5 in Notes from Nowhere (ed.), *We are Everywhere* (London: Verso, 2003).

2 Linden Farrer, 'Dance Around the G8: Pink Silver, Pink, and Silver: Contested Identities Against the G8', 2002. Dissertation summary at <www.pcworks.demon.co.uk/magazine/campaign/ pinksilver.htm>

3 <www.antenna.nl/organicchaos/PinkSilver/PSindex.html>

4 Farrer, 'Dance Around the G8'.

5 Ibid.

6 'Rhythms of Resistance', SchNEWS of the World, Yearbook, 2002.

7 Pink & Silver Index at <www.antenna.nl/organicchaos/ PinkSilver/PSindex.html>

8 Call on Toronto police radio on date of first Global Street Party, May 1998.

9 Farrer, 'Dance Around the G8'.

10 Notes from Nowhere, 'Walking: We Ask Questions', in *We are Everywhere*, p. 506.

27 Lee Kyung-Hae, organizer of farmers in South Korea and member of Vía Campesina, on his way to the fence preventing access to the WTO 5th Ministerial in Cancún, Mexico, 10 September 2003 (image from Activist Media Project, *This is What Free Trade Looks Like* [documentary film] 2004, camera: Sabin Portillo)

27 | Suicide: like a lamp

Suicide is a rare political event, but nevertheless one with a strong tradition. Hardly encouraged by activists, suicide is one of a few tactics with incredible catalysing power. At the same time, many political suicides go entirely unnoticed. Unlike tactics which disrupt, create alternatives or educate, 'politically inspired suicides are dramatic, public acts intended to send symbolic messages that will challenge shared values and stir the consciousness of the public',[1] urging people to take action against their oppression. '"I will open my eyes in the other world and watch you march with a smile. On the day of victory, I will send you fervent silent applause that will move the whole world!" ... Sang-jin Kim (1975) ... envisioned that a new democratic society with freedom and equality would be promoted by his sacrifice.'[2]

The most famous twentieth-century political suicide was that of Thich Quang Duc, a Vietnamese Buddhist monk protesting religious persecution under the Diem regime. Following his act in June 1963, other Vietnamese monks and nuns, Sri Lankans, Indians, Czechs, as well as Americans protesting the war against Vietnam, adopted the tactic,[3] creating a modern model for 'using their bodies like a lamp for help'.[4]

Political suicide is an ancient form of protest, and Quang Duc's became an international symbol. The act and its presentation were modernized. A procession of well-organized monks produced a fake stalled car in order to take over a road junction for the protest, blocked fire engines by laying down under the wheels, alerted the press and provided clear explanations in English.

While some scholars believe that all modern political immolations derive from Quang Duc, there are long lineages of historical precedents including African slaves, Japanese ritual suicides, Russian refugees as they were being repatriated, miserable wives, and quite a tradition of Buddhist monks.[5] Korea has had a particularly strong tradition in the modern era. During the Japanese occupation, a number of prominent scholars committed suicide in 1905, leading to increased resistance to the occupation. In 1970, a Korean designer committed suicide to protest sweatshop conditions, leading to a strengthened and more democratic labour movement independent of the government.

Generally, governments marginalize political suicides, claiming that the activists had personal or psychological problems. But the political history of the activists, along with testimony of their family and friends, reveal that most such suicides are 'highly symbolic acts ... carefully premeditated, often for long periods of time'.[6]

Peace Teams are organized to bring outsiders into war zones to provide witnesses in the hope of leveraging their Global North privilege as a form of shield. Central American Peace Teams used this tactic in the 1980s and the International Solidarity Movement is currently one such group working in Palestine. This tactic is sometimes understood as part of the tradition of self-sacrifice in which foreign civilian witnesses and sometimes journalists intentionally risk their lives. This tradition of active pacifism[7] can be seen as a readiness for political suicide.[8] Several international activists in Palestine have been killed or seriously injured in recent years while blocking Israeli army actions, including Rachel Corrie (aged twenty-three, from the USA) and Tom Hurndall (twenty-one, from the UK).[9]

On 10 September 2003, farmer and organizer Lee Kyung-Hae, wearing the sign 'WTO! Kills. Farmers', climbed the fence surrounding the Cancún WTO Ministerial and stabbed himself. Lee Kyung's sacrifice was the first immolation recognized internationally in the style of Quang Duc as part of the alterglobalization movement. In truth, it was not as singular as it seemed.

The indigenous U'wa people had threatened to commit mass suicide in 1995 if Occidental Petroleum with the collaboration of the Colombian government continued its attempts to drill on their land. This was one of the opening salvos from the emerging international anti-corporate movement.

In the municipality of Güicán, department of Boyacá ... a hundred of our ancestors ... instead of being subjugated to the Spanish laws and authorities ... decided to die throwing themselves from the highest part of this cliff down to the most silent void – that with its surrounding natural environment received the bodies and sacred spirits of these heroes.

This historic fact – to die rather than submit to and be destroyed by the enemies – defines the decision of our ancestors to commit collective suicide to preserve the secrets of the U'wa culture. All of this [was done] with a sense of spiritual strength, cultural zeal and dignity of a people that has always resisted changing the natural and cultural wealth that governs our *cosmovisión* and cosmology, [and] defining the road of autonomy and cultural identity ... Our position today in 2003 has not changed and cannot change because it would violate our internal constitutional legal system and other laws of origin and of cultural survival.[10]

Emerging from the militant Korean movements against trade liberalization and structural adjustment, six Korean labour leaders committed suicide between January 2003 and February 2004. New laws had been passed holding union leaders responsible for financial damage caused by labour actions.[11] In late 2003, nine immigrant workers committed suicide to protest the government's deportation plan.

Since 1995, a highly contested number of farmers in several Indian states have committed suicide protesting trade policies, introduction of biotech seeds and lack of government support for farmers who are in crisis as a result of these policies.[12] British farmers are killing themselves at the rate of one per week, while US farmers kill themselves at three times the normal suicide rate of the rest of the population. In Korea, with the implementation of trade liberalization in agriculture, nearly half of all farmers have been driven out of business. Around

In memory of Lee Kyung Hae and all the farmers killed by corporate globalization and WTO policies.

Memorial, 11 September 2003
Plaza de la Reforma, Cancún, Mexico

20 per cent of all Korean suicides use pesticides.[13] The highly toxic and easily available paraquat is popularly used in the 1–2 million intentional pesticide poisonings each year in the Global South.[14]

Quang Duc established suicide as a spiritual, non-violent, moral political statement. Lee Kyung politicized the routine despair of farmers who commit suicide to escape the shame of debt and failure despite their hard work. These complex cries of suffering and inspiration include 125,000 rural Chinese women who commit suicide with pesticides each year,[15] teenagers in southern India,[16] prison suicides and other ordinary suicides linked to political oppression. Lee Kyung's activism expressed a 'desire to light up the history and make visible the suffering' of peasants, women and youth whose political voices, even in this most costly register, are routinely ignored.[17]

Resource

Lee Kyung Hae's statement to the WTO: <www.americaspolicy. org/columns/amprog/2003/0309lee.html>

Notes

1 B. C. Ben Park, 'Self-immolation and Suicide Attacks: An Interpretive Approach to Self-destruction as a Political Act Among the Young', conference on A Global Perspective on Problems of Identity Development and Suicide in Indigenous Minority Youth, Bellagio Study and Conference Centre, Italy, 28 June to 3 July 2004.

2 Ibid.

3 The first evidence of diffusion outside Vietnam was a Sinhalese nurse in Sri Lanka, who jumped from a building making explicit reference to Quang Duc to raise attention to an ongoing

strike just days after his immolation. Tamils in Sri Lanka quickly adopted the tactic. By the end of 1965, three US citizens had self-immolated in their struggle to end the Vietnam War. In 1969, Jan Palach set fire to himself to urge his fellow Czechs to resist Soviet occupation and censorship and to protect democracy. Other Czechs followed. This form of protest continues in Vietnam to the present day. In September 2001, Ho Tan Anh set himself on fire protesting religious persecution. Michael Biggs attempts a global review of the tradition in 'Dying without Killing: Protest by Self-Immolation', in Diego Gambetta (ed.), *Making Sense of Suicide Missions* (Oxford: Oxford University Press, 2004).

4 Thich Thien-An (1975) in ibid.

5 Academic studies of self-immolation are few. Most focus on debating the religious meaning and acceptability of the act. See Russell T. McCutcheon, *Manufacturing Religion* (Oxford: Oxford University Press, 1997) for a discussion of this tendency. Biggs, op. cit., examines only 533 acts after 1963, excluding those not covered on global newswires and all prison suicides.

6 Park, 'Self-immolation'.

7 Ward Churchill argues that privileged pacifists should oppose war by intervening with their own bodies. See *Pacifism as Pathology* (Winnipeg: Arbeiter Ring, 1986, 1998).

8 Marianne Arbogast, 'Dying for Change: Self-Sacrifice in Nonviolent Action', *Witness for Peace* magazine (May/June 2003), <www.thewitness.org> Activist witnesses and accompaniments have worked in Central America since the early 1980s.

9 See <www.rachelcorrie.org> and <www.tomhurndall.co.uk>

10 Roberto Afanador Cobaria-Berito Kubaruwa, 'U'wa: Collective Suicide: Association of U'wa Traditional Authorities', *OneWorld*, 10 March 2003, at <www.globalpolicy.org/nations/sovereign/sover/emerg/2003/0731uwa.htm>

11 Soh Ji-young, 'Unions Rail Against "Unjust" Suits Lodged by Employers', *Korea Times*, 26 October 2003.

12 Vandana Shiva claims that 25,000 farmers have commited suicide in India since 1997. See 'The Suicide Economy of Corporate Globalisation', *Znet*, 19 February 2004 at <www.zmag.org> News reports document numbers closer to a total of 1,000. Also see R. M. Vidyasagar and K. Suman Chandra, 'Farmers' Suicides in Andhra Pradesh and Karnataka', Centre for Social Development, National Institute of Rural Development,

Hyderabad, April 2003. On the politicization of Indian farmers' suicides, see 'Farmers' Suicide and Farmers' Rights', resolution passed by the Forum of Farmers' Organizations on Globalization and Agriculture in the National Workshop on Globalization of Agriculture and the Survival of Small and Marginal Peasants held at the Constitution Club, New Delhi, 30 May 1998, online at <www.vshiva.net/archives/campaigns/suicide&rights.htm>. The political meaning of suicide in India is indicated by its use by a broad range of activists who have exhausted other methods of protest. Activist group suicides have included Sikh widows of riot victims, high-caste persons opposing university set-asides for lower-castes, oppressed Tamils and members of marginal parties denied access to the ballot.

13 Kyu-Yoon Hwang, Eun-Young Lee and Sae-Yong Hong, 'Paraquat Intoxication in Korea', *Archives of Environmental Health*, March–April 2002.

14 Pestizid Aktions-Netzwerk e.V. (PAN Germany), 'Paraquat and Suicide: Fact Sheet 2003', at <www.pan-germany.org> Some analysts blame these deaths on neurological imbalances caused by pesticide poisoning in 'normal' use.

15 Reuters, 'Pesticide Suicides in China Kill 125,000 Annually', 1 November 2001.

16 Shaoni Bhattacharya, 'Indian Teens Have World's Highest Suicide Rate', *New Scientist*, April 2004, at <newscientist.com>

17 Bill Wylie-Kellermann in Marianne Arbogast, 'Dying for Change: Self-sacrifice in Nonviolent Action', *Satya*, April 2004 at <www.satyamag.com>

28 | Conclusion: Globalize this! We are winning

How is it remotely possible that these few activists perceive that they are winning? They are delusional. Isn't it clear that Nike and Citicorp are winning? Don't most economics experts support globalization? Aren't its proponents backed with frightening military power and the weight of history? The stories of resistance must be exaggerated.

How can we be winning, as people are beaten and jailed and bombed all over the world? What on earth can it mean for careful, respected scholars such as Noam Chomsky to pronounce: 'So we have won. There is nothing left for us to do but pick up the pieces – not only to talk about a vision of the future that is just and humane, but to move on to create it.'[1]

Worried elites

The power of the movement was acknowledged by its bitter enemies several years ago. In 2000, a former US official at the Trilateral Commission announced: 'All the momentum is with the anti-globalization forces.'[2] Neoliberal publications worried:

The protesters are right that the most pressing moral, political and economic issue of our time is third-world poverty. And they are right that the tide of 'globalization', powerful as the engines driving it may be, can be turned back. The fact that both these things are true is what makes the protesters – and, crucially, the strand of popular opinion that sympathizes with them – so terribly dangerous. International economic integration is not an ineluctable process ... It is only one, the best, of many possible futures for the world economy; others may be chosen, are even coming to seem more likely ... The protesters are right that governments and companies – if only they can be moved by force of argument, or just by force – have it within

28 Zapatista women storm San Cristóbal de las Casas, Chiapas, Mexico, to demand that indigenous women's rights be respected (photo by Tim Russo)

their power to slow and even reverse the economic trends of the past 20 years ... The mighty forces driving globalization are surely, you might think, impervious to the petty aggravation of street protesters wearing silly costumes. Certainly, one would have hoped so, but it is proving otherwise.[3]

Since elites started wringing their hands, the movement has only become more focused and organized with the development of the World Social Forum and many other networks of cooperation and coordination. 'Whereas the neoliberal paradigm was completely hegemonic up to a few years ago, now it is strongly challenged, as you can see from the widespread reception of the Fitoussi Report.'[4]

Reforms and cooptation

Institutional victories include several of the G8 cancelling bilateral debt with poor countries as well as immanent multilateral action to cancel debts owed to the World Bank and IMF. Tobin-type currency taxation laws are rapidly gaining credibility, and have already been passed by several countries.[5]

Codes of conduct and industry self-monitoring organizations such as the Fair Labor Association are totally inadequate as a method of eliminating sweatshops, but they are a good measure of the power of anti-sweatshop movements which have successfully embarrassed and damaged the images of the most famous fashion manufacturers. Cooptation and reforms testify to the growing strength of the alterglobalization movement.

Political consciousness

Dispersed movements are progressively more able to connect local problems with wider struggles against globalization. The analytic coherence of the movement is accompanied by forms of organization which, although perpetually frustrating to socialists, have proven robust. Working to increase collaboration while also minimizing hierarchy is surely slow going. By protecting autonomy, the movement of movements has constrained both marginalization and elitism and has not been fooled by cooptation.

We are winning

255

While 'anti-terrorist' policies have criminalized the alter-globalization movement, 9/11 also greatly strengthened the movement. The attempts to pre-empt wars and end occupation are not only unprecedented but also deeply informed by the struggle against neoliberalism advanced by the alterglobalization movement in the preceding years. 9/11 and its aftermath greatly strengthened the popular understanding of neoliberalism as fundamentally imperialist.

Local struggles

Building 'another world' is well under way. Opposition to ministerials and summits is ongoing. At the same time, local conflicts are becoming more entrenched as the struggle deepens. After a stunning and inspiring victory against water privatization, Bechtel, the World Bank and the Bolivian government, the Coordinadora del Agua y la Vida in Cochabamba has got down to the business of administrating the local water system.

Meanwhile in early 2005 a second water contract is cancelled in El Alto, under pressure of another 'water revolt' and another president of Bolivia is actually being held accountable, by an unprecedented and militant coalition of 'all the social movements', to retain national control over hydrocarbons. Uruguayans break 170 years of right-wing political power to elect a left president in order to address the rapid impoverization of more than 30 per cent of the population under neoliberalism. The Zapatistas are building regional 'good governments' and enforcing the Women's Revolutionary Law. The Brazilian Movimento dos Rurais Sem Terra produces beans and rice for Lula's anti-hunger programme, and participates in the creation of a National Plan for Agrarian Reform.

Every day the hundreds of thousands of communities joining the revolt take small steps away from corporations and their governments by inventing independent justice, trade, law or communication. People in Guerrero, Mexico, have implemented community policing and alternative sentencing. The World Tribunal on Iraq, beginning with the Brussels Tribunal in April 2004, moves forward with the people's agenda, regardless of the lack of cooperation of their representatives. People build Fair Trade networks or get to know nearby farmers. IndyMedia activists come to town to get people involved with the movement's media and help out with the local radio station.

Still building a global movement

In 2004 the People's Caravan for Food Sovereignty walked in the footsteps of the 1998 Peoples' Global Action Intercontinental Caravan of Solidarity and Resistance. The ongoing process of organizing includes enticing more people to participate in their own future, to develop new kinds of organizations (and nonorganizations), and to build global networks (without allowing for the emergence of bureaucracies and elites). Each small (and frustratingly time-consuming) piece of work in decolonization creates the new world, by expanding the space within which all who have been marginalized can work.

The movements, for the most part, are not aiming to take state power. Instead, they seek to build other forms of power, autonomous power to solve their own problems and independent power to compel direct accountability from international institutions, corporations and the state. The movements are resolutely distrustful of elites (*que se vayan todos!*) and often refuse to compromise or negotiate. This is an expansive intransigence, continually embracing more issues and struggles (rather than narrowing the focus).

> From the moment that governments or political parties calling themselves democratic were no longer able to reassure people or give them answers – that was when people started to take direct action ... people ... who admitted they had not been active for twenty years [found] renewed confidence in the possibility of changing things ... each new rally holds out hope, is proof that the worldwide challenge is being maintained ... It's an odd sort of militancy ... The number of requests from non-farmers to join the Farmers' Confederation is further evidence

of what's happening ... a huge movement, but with no desire to take power ... people mobilize without wanting to take over state institutions ... beyond the traditional parties. Politics is given a new credibility.[6]

Understanding fully the limitations of ecology, modernization fantasies, and benevolent elites, every day we come to realize in more detail the capabilities of our communities, our creativity, and the necessity of solidarity in defence of diversity and self-determination. 'Our blood and our word have lit a small fire in the mountain and we walk a path against the house of money and the powerful. Brothers and sisters of other races and languages, of other colors, but with the same heart now protect our light and in it they drink of the same fire.'[7]

And you?

Notes

1 Noam Chomsky, 'Confronting the Empire', World Social Forum, 3 February 2003. 'In Davos,' the *New York Times* tells us, 'the mood has darkened'. For the 'movers and shakers' it is not 'global party time' any more. In fact, the founder of the [World Economic] Forum has conceded defeat: 'The power of corporations has completely disappeared,' he said.

2 C. Fred Bergsten (Director, Institute for International Economics, former US Assistant Secretary of the Treasury for International Affairs), 'The Backlash Against Globalization', Trilateral Commission, annual meeting, Tokyo, 2000, at <www.trilateral.org>

3 Opinion (no author), 'The Case for Globalization', *The Economist*, 21 September 2000.

4 Bernard Cassen, 'Inventing ATTAC' (January 2003), pp. 152–74 in Tom Mertes (ed.), *A Movement of Movements: Is Another World Really Possible?* (London: Verso, 2004).

5 For updates see <www.tobintaxireland.ie/international_govs.html>

6 José Bové in José Bové and François Dufour with Gilles Luneau, *The World is not for Sale: Farmers Against Junk Food*, trans. Anna de Casparis (London: Verso, 2002), pp. 185–88.

7 Fourth Declaration of the Lacandon Jungle, 1 January 1996.

Index